CUE
THE
LIFEBOAT

CUE
THE
LIFEBOAT

A Choose-Your-Current Guide
to Get Your Ship Together

CHRISTIANE PALPANT

Ripples Media

Published by Ripples Media
Atlanta, Georgia
www.ripples.media

For more information: contact@ripples.media

First printing 2026

Book and cover design by Burtch Hunter

ISBN 978-1-971718-09-5 (Paperback)
ISBN 978-1-971718-10-1 (Hardcover)
ISBN 978-1-971718-08-8 (eBook)

Library of Congress Control Number: 2026907216

To my little-sissy-bossy-pants.
Your unwavering support has been my anchor and my compass.

To my Georgia State Professional Sales Students.
I'm so impressed with your grit, determination, and courage.
Keep going!

To Heather and Ripples.
Your generous listening and boundless creativity
gave this book its wings.

WORDS FROM THE FORWARD CREW
A.K.A. FOREWORD

*Why these stories were written for you
and worth absorbing. Dive In!*

FIRST LAUNCH
Voices from the Start of the Journey

. . .

Beneath the detailed stories lie mental dilemmas every reader will one day wrestle with. I could see myself in every character's journey, even in worlds I've never known.

CAMPBELL MILES, RECENT GRADUATE, CONTINUING IMMERSIVE INTERNATIONAL TRAVEL AND CROSS-CULTURAL EDUCATION

Cue the Lifeboat is a thoughtful companion for moments when life seems unclear. This is a book that I would highly recommend to anyone who feels as if they are overwhelmed in their current stage of life.

DYLAN CROSS, COLLEGE STUDENT, BALANCING ACADEMICS WITH A FULL-TIME PROFESSIONAL ROLE

I picked this up right after graduating, when I was feeling lost, scared, and unsure about what comes next. It honestly was exactly what I needed.

SARA DOYLE, RECENT GRADUATE

In a season where overwhelming feelings can take over quickly, this book has been a fabulous reality check. It's a primer that met me right where I'm at, on MY timeline. Reading it felt like permission to stop panicking and loosen my grip.

RACHELLE ALMAZAN, FUTURE GRADUATE

A wonderfully crafted adventure book, a deep dive not only shown as a guide for young adults charting transitional phases in their lives, but also an autobiography of the author herself and the wisdom she has gained and poured into this book!

JOSEPH D. SMITH II, POET AND UNIVERSITY STUDENT

This phenomenal choose-your-own-journey unfolds differently each time you return to it, offering perspective, reassurance, and direction for early professionals finding their footing through life's biggest transitions.

SHIV SHARMA, GRADUATE AND EARLY PROFESSIONAL ENTREPRENEUR

Through honest stories and practical lessons that you can reflect on, it offers reassurance that setbacks, uncertainty, and pauses are part of growth, not signs of failure.

CRISTIAN MALDONADO, RECENT GRADUATE AND SALES CLUB FOUNDER

FINDING BEARINGS
Perspectives from the Open Water

. . .

Your journey is unique, but Christiane proves you don't have to take on the world alone. Don't be worried about taking the wrong step or a step back, because the biggest accomplishment is to keep moving.

REBECCA E. THOMAS, ACTIVATOR AND BUILDER OF ENDURING, IMPACTFUL RELATIONSHIPS

For the 25 years I have known Christiane, she has been a passionate, energetic, and deeply committed advocate for young people. She has a rare ability to help them cast a vision for a future broader and more meaningful than they imagined. Christiane brings both wisdom and real-world insight to the critical transition from college into the professional world. Her guidance is grounded, hopeful, and uniquely suited to those standing at the threshold of what comes next.

MAGGIE PHILPOTTS, MENTEE OF THE AUTHOR FOR MORE THAN TWO DECADES

Author, and one of the most interesting people I know, CP invites you to take the helm as protagonist sharing in her adventure while encouraging you to reflect on the universal lessons learned along the way. Perhaps the most important of all: life's a journey, enjoy the ride.

HEATHER SUMPERL, EDITOR, ADMINISTRATIVE DIRECTOR, ADVENTURE SEEKER

Every chapter seems to connect perfectly to a different area of my life, encouraging me to dream bigger and ultimately to trust myself, knowing that when all else fails, I can always pivot.

ALLISON PETERKA, OCCUPATIONAL THERAPIST

As someone early in my own career, I found this to be a thoroughly effective life guide, with a unique structure that leverages the power of stories to contextualize its lessons.

TONY SHIMKETS, ASSOCIATE PROJECT MANAGER

Christiane Palpant is the person everyone wants to be when they grow up. Smart, beautifully spoken, insightful, and adventurous. She is an inspiration to all who know her. And now, she's written a road-map showing us all how to forge a path to destiny!

RIVKEH SAHLIN, VICE PRESIDENT OF SALES, MOTHER OF BOYS & CHAMPION OF WOMEN

READING THE CURRENT
Guidance Earned Through Experience

. . .

I wish I'd had this guidebook as a recent college graduate, unsure of my next steps. Although now, as a seasoned professional embarking on a career reinvention, the advice is just as pertinent. I couldn't put down my pencil, constantly circling, underlining, and writing "yes!" in the margins.

AMY SWEEZEY, AUTHOR, SPEAKER, METEOROLOGIST, AND PODCAST HOST OF *REINVENTION AT ANY AGE*

Meet the voice as colorful and open-hearted as the stories she tells. Driven by fearless curiosity, she embraces life's twists to create heart-led adventures that invite readers to see the world differently. If you're ready to discover hidden opportunities and open your own doors, this is the author to follow.

KIMBER SHRAY, VICE PRESIDENT MARKETING

With its ingenious choose-your-own-adventure format, Cue the Lifeboat *meets young adults exactly where they are and empowers them to navigate uncertainty with confidence, curiosity, and purpose. Its Propeller Plans and Choose Your Current prompts don't just inspire reflection, they ignite momentum while contextualizing "failure," making this an essential, life-shaping guide for anyone designing a future they truly love.*

RICHARD SHIMKETS, PH.D. AND CEO

This book challenges the reader to embrace all their experiences and reflect on them with kindness and a fresh perspective. It makes the reader the captain to live their best life, not a victim of circumstance.

AMY EVINS, CHIEF INFORMATION TECHNOLOGY OFFICER

This is a field guide, still wet and sandy, like the journals of Lewis and Clark, written in the voice of an intrepid adventurer and pioneer who doesn't just help show you the way but empowers you to see all the options, and makes it look fun.

APRIL ARMSTRONG, AUTHOR OF *THE DAY ONE EXECUTIVE: A GUIDEBOOK TO STAND OUT IN YOUR CAREER STARTING NOW*

After reading Cue the Lifeboat, *I am convinced that whether you are a new college graduate, a brand new parent, or a mid-career professional looking for the courage to make a job change, you will find comfort and direction within the pages of this book.*

MATT SINKOVITZ, FINANCIAL SERVICES EXECUTIVE AND OWNER OF SINK'S GARAGE

For graduates asking, "now what?," this book delivers clarity. A choose-your-own roadmap for purpose, direction, and momentum.

PHIL EVERHART, PRESIDENT AND FOUNDER OF SMARTFOX TECHNOLOGIES

Christiane is not afraid to be vulnerable and reveal some hard experiences from her life which could help others to find strength in their struggles and rise from the ashes of lost battles, discouragement, and defeat.

NATALIA SHABLIA, UNIVERSITY DIRECTOR OF SPONSORED RESEARCH AND ORGANIZATIONAL LEADER WHO SUPPORTS SPECIAL NEEDS ORPHANS IN UKRAINE

Cue the Lifeboat feels like a steady, trusted companion for those moments when life stops being linear. It meets you exactly where you are, blending real-life stories with practical insight that helps you trust yourself as you figure out what's next. This is a book you don't just read once; you come back to it whenever you need clarity, courage, or direction.

HELEN HALLORAN, FINANCIAL SERVICES LEADER

Cue the Lifeboat is the book I wish I'd had at the start of my career! Palpant offers up real world lessons and practical wisdom from an over 30-year business career while being in sync with the current moment as business school professor to thousands of university students. She has been listening to the challenges, frustrations, and questions of Millennials and Gen Z as they enter the real world. It is a book truly made for this time.

REBECCA SHIMKETS, M.S., PUBLIC AND MENTAL HEALTH CONSULTANT AND WRITER

If choose-your-own-adventure could be a person, it would be Christiane. I have known this amazing human for over 30 years and have never met another one like her. She has zest! She has enthusiasm! She has smarts and empathy! Christiane is a positive bright light in this world and wants everyone to succeed.

PAULA J. A. MCNALLY, PH.D., INSTRUCTOR AT LUDDY SCHOOL OF INFORMATICS, COMPUTING, AND ENGINEERING, AND LONGTIME FRIEND OF THE AUTHOR

I loved the unique way that you can navigate the chapters based on the needs of the moment all while traveling around the globe.

JOELLE GRACIA, FOUNDER OF MEET ME IN PARIS

Christiane is one of the most authentic and grounded human beings I know—while living in the Western world, specifically in America, she is a true citizen of the world. Her depth of life and near-death experiences have given her the unique empowered position to share her forged insights with the rest of us, especially the next generation of young adults, like few can.

ALEXANDRA LEEVEN WAGNER, SENIOR BRAND MARKETER

Friendship with Christiane is a choose-your-own adventure. From college classrooms to cross-country road trips, from shared laughter to real challenges, she has a rare way of turning everyday moments into meaningful stories. I've watched her take creative risks, embrace new ideas, and meet life's twists with curiosity and courage. When life gives you the chance to choose your own adventure, choosing Christiane is always the right call.

ESTHER HARVEY, COLLEGE ROOMMATE AND LIFELONG FRIEND

Christiane has been a dear friend of mine for over 25 years and has consistently shown up when I've needed support, regardless of what was happening in her own life. She is deeply unselfish, genuinely cares for those around her, and inspires complete trust.

DEBBIE SMITH, SENIOR VICE PRESIDENT AT A LARGE, FULL-SERVICE INVESTMENT FIRM

LIGHTING THE WAY
Reflections from Seasoned Navigators

. . .

Cue the Lifeboat *is a work of rare tonal precision—an intimate, clear-eyed book of nonfiction that resists easy categorization. Through brief, carefully structured pieces drawn from personal everyday encounters, travel, and lived experience, Christiane Palpant examines moments of kindness and ethical choice with restraint and clarity, never resorting to spectacle or sentimentality. The lifeboat here is not rescue but attention: a disciplined practice of noticing, naming, and staying present when the stakes are real, and certainty is unavailable.*

P. ROBERTO GARCIA, PH.D., DISTINGUISHED CLINICAL PROFESSOR OF INTERNATIONAL BUSINESS, KELLEY SCHOOL OF BUSINESS, INDIANA UNIVERSITY

Cue the Lifeboat *is a hugely enjoyable read for anyone seeking a fresh way to look at career options ahead. You never know where the author will take you next as readers contemplate a series of thought provoking questions to guide them on their personal and professional journey.*

KEN SCHROEDER, ASSOCIATE CHAIR, DEPARTMENT OF MARKETING, GEORGIA STATE UNIVERSITY

In her book, Cue the Lifeboat, *Christiane Palpant delivers a truly innovative and engaging book that transforms professional development into an immersive, choose-your-own-adventure experience without ever losing the reader's attention. Her ability to present critical, real-world career lessons in such an exciting and accessible way sets this book apart.*

DEREK VALENTINE, PROFESSOR AT CLARK ATLANTA UNIVERSITY

Professor CP's book helps readers uncover their authentic selves while making thoughtful choices about career, purpose, and life direction. It's an encouraging companion for anyone ready to step forward with self-trust and intention.

MARK BROOKS, PH.D., CLINICAL NEUROPSYCHOLOGIST

A fantastic piece of literature. I experienced every emotion while reading it. Authentic, honest, and raw. Some of the best life lessons. May others use these lessons as guide posts for their journey.

TODD BAILEY, FORMER BANK CHIEF FINANCIAL OFFICER

The thought provoking questions help you evaluate where you are and navigate to where you want to be whether it is a big life change or a small tweak. I highly recommend this read for all ages and plan to read it again and again to keep my compass aligned.

MARY PETERKA, FORMER FINANCIAL SERVICES EXECUTIVE AND THE AUTHOR'S QUADRUPLE COLLEAGUE

You'll be able to explore and define who you are, who else and what essentials you need with you to navigate the journey to each new career destination with confidence, crewmates, and joy!

KRISTEN J. ALEXANDER, FORMER FINTECH AND FINOPS LEADER

A unique format that pulls readers in as they explore how to navigate in the everyday world. It's a book to read and reread for charting your course in life!

SHIRLENE BROOKS, AWARD WINNING INTERIOR DESIGNER AND ENTREPRENEUR

Synthesizing life's journey and finding a way to reinvent yourself is CP's superpower. Throughout many years of friendship, she has modeled for me how to embrace what life gives you and roll with it. To welcome whatever shows up at your door, whether challenging or joyful, and harmonize it with your life.

Z. GILMAN, THREE DECADES NAVIGATING FINANCIAL MARKETS, NOW TENDING MINDFULNESS AND INTENTIONAL LIVING

CUE
THE
LIFEBOAT

CONTENTS

⚓

SECTION I

Casting Off

THE LEAP INTO OPEN WATERS

Preparing:
Your Pre-Departure Checklist

Life is not linear for everyone!
GARRETT G.

School moves like a hallway in straight lines.
Real life swerves like a stormy sea.
This guidebook will help you navigate the chaos of your
wild, crazy and complex journey through life.
Cue the lifeboat!

The black four-cornered cap flies higher and higher into the air with the tassel leading the way, almost like a shooting star paving a path toward your future. With the graduation march song "Pomp and Circumstance" still whirring, you take one last look at everything you know on the deck of your predictable cruise liner coasting effortlessly on the surface of a bottomless sea.

Hoisting your black gown above your ankles, you grip the steel ladder that drops from the deck to the waterline, ending at a slender diving board hanging like a cliff over the open ocean. In the distance are barely visible dots of your fellow students who have made the jump and are looking for their own lifeboats. Your toes brush the end of the board as you prepare your dive into the unknown.

Out of a vacuum, your vision expands, and you snap back to your surroundings.

Your daydream disappears and with sweaty palms you rip the image of the graduates, the boat, a diving board, and the open sea out of the magazine you are reading. This visual haunts you because you hold a nautical knot of emotions in your gut about diving from the safety of your figurative boat into a sea of unknown.

A mix of anticipation and nausea churns in your stomach, urging you to save the powerful image. You reach for your backpack, searching for the notebook that's become your trusted companion.

You distinctly remember the moment three and a half years ago when your Grandfather Muse gave you the heirloom notebook.

He was propped up against a stack of pillows. You were taken by the depth of wisdom and peace in his face; his eyes still had the twinkle of his mischievous younger self. You sat beside the bed, unsure whether to treat the moment like an ending. He didn't.

"You're going to need this," he said, tapping the cover of the book. Not dramatic, not ceremonial, just matter of fact, the way he gave most of his best advice.

His hand met yours and, in that moment, he entrusted you with what he called his "compass rose," the cover of the notebook etched with the arrows pointing due north. Below, the printed words, *"Aude Volāre."*

You weren't sure what that meant, but it seemed important.

He watched you study the notebook, sensing puzzlement, but sure certainty would follow.

His eyes met yours and he uttered the words from the cover, *"Aude Volāre."*

His voice was steady, the room quiet. Nothing heavy. No long speeches. Just the kind of exchange the two of you always had—simple, direct, and strangely inspiring.

Accepting the notebook didn't feel like a farewell, but rather an assignment he expected you to carry forward.

It is this moment that returns to you now: not the shadows of the day, but the clarity of his intention and the confidence that you were ready for what would come next.

You thoughtfully place the torn comic of the graduate, boat and diving board between pages of the treasured notebook that has never left your side since Grandfather Muse charged you with it.

. . .

Diving from the mother ship into the waves of life's roaring sea was a choppy experience for me. Following a long career in corporate management, I am now a professor and am once again standing at the base of the ladder on the ship. This time I am preparing students to jump into the vast ocean of real life.

I've now had the privilege of hearing more than a thousand students share their thoughts and expectations about the journey ahead. Students use words such as stress, anxiety, unknown, uncharted, bewildered, mental illness, depression, and imposter syndrome to describe their feelings of the journey that awaits them.

Relatable?

After twelve to sixteen predictable and linear years of schooling, the system seems to push you off the edge, "Here's your diploma, sink or swim!"

Once you dive into the open water, you'll find there is no personal flotation device or life jacket to prevent you from swallowing too much saltwater or refuge to keep hungry sea creatures from feasting on your feet.

Cue the Lifeboat!

This book is your guide to finding deep and meaningful principles that will carry you through times of significant change with actionable plans that can alter not only your present state but the trajectory of your life.

*Each story in these pages is drawn from real experiences
taken from my own life, moments where my lessons
proved both sharp and unforgettable.
Following in my footsteps, you will board planes, trains,
boats and automobiles to walk in my shoes through
diverse experiences from around the world.*

You are the main character of these stories, and will engage in rich adventures that will help to keep you afloat and propel you toward meaningful direction in your own life.

MAP OF DESTINATIONS BY CHAPTERS

Take note: life is not linear and, therefore, this content is not linear. The word "linear" implies progressing from one stage to another in a straight line, much like the structure of a classroom or the progression from one grade to the next. Because life is not linear, school can be an inaccurate (and often ill-equipped) training ground for what's to come.

Change is inevitable, but this text offers tools that will enable you to handle seismic shifts before your literal next chapter in life. Not only is this content useful for a recent graduate entering the workforce for the first time, the principles are also meaningful for those needing to make a change or build momentum. This content can be helpful throughout many different stages of life:

- *Graduating high school or university*
- *Deciding about trade school or entrepreneurship*
- *Segueing from military to civilian life*
- *Considering a mid-career pivot*
- *Discovering a new chapter after a divorce or loss of a loved one or partner.*

Mimicking our non-linear life, you are welcome to consume this content in any order you desire. With that said, it is helpful to start from the beginning to set your course and build on your vision. Then, you are free to choose the direction you will take from two scenarios presented at the end of each chapter.

If you would like to plot your journey, simply "check the box" after reading each chapter.

As a side note, for those listening to this content while driving, until we have autonomous cars, you can relax into the flow and listen to the content in sequential order.

Just like starting over in life, this content can be restarted and experienced in a different order. It's your path, and therefore, your choice.

Choose your chapter, choose your path, choose your future.

~ SET YOUR SAILS ~

A SAMPLE GUIDE FOR INTERACTIVE CHAPTER FLOW

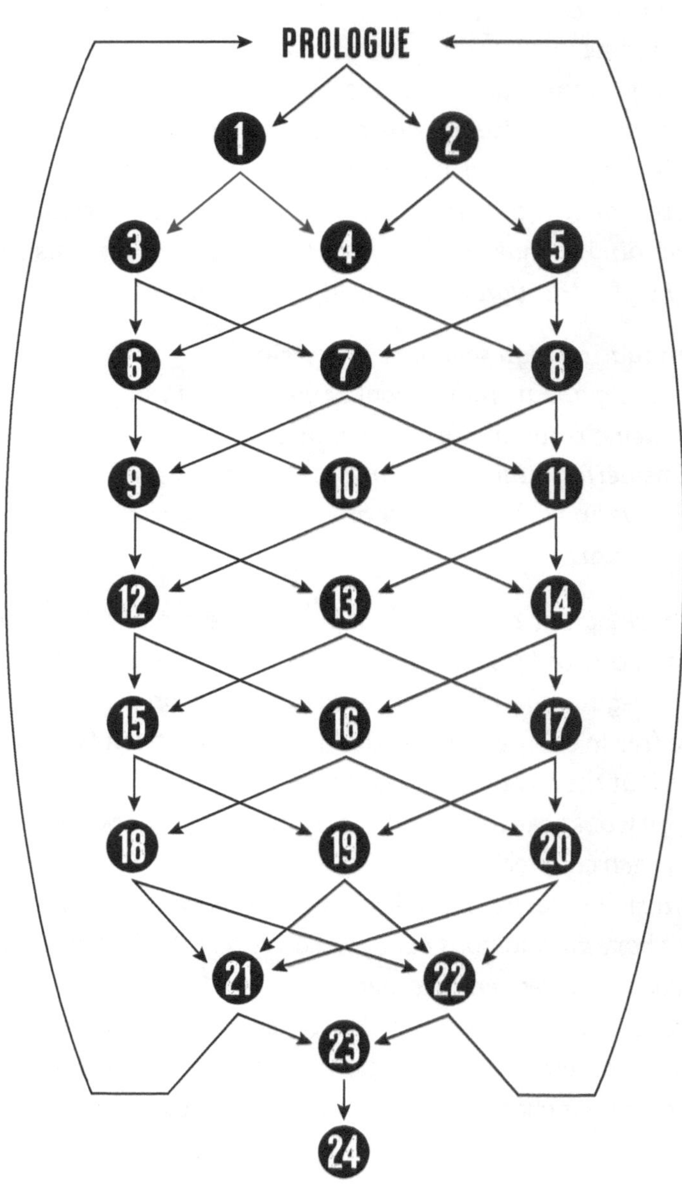

No matter which chapter you choose to read within a section, you will gather vital information for that stage in your journey. Don't worry about understanding the flow right now, the characters you meet within the chapters will help guide you.

To punctuate your learning and experience, at the end of each chapter there are two short but important elements that will impact your journey:

The Propeller Plan *is your momentum moment. This exercise at the end of each chapter leaves you with points to ponder, tasks to try, and words of encouragement that will help you launch toward a meaningful direction.*

Choose-Your-Current™ *guides the direction of your next reading. Your course of discovery will take you through stormy seas, ask you to find depth within, and trust in the mentors you meet along the way.*

During your journey through the chapters . . . you are led by the wisdom of this navigation guide, but the direction is in your own hands. The ride will be turbulent, but I guarantee it will be thrilling.

Dive in.

CHOOSE-YOUR-CURRENT

As you begin your journey, you run your fingers over the ancient seal on the front cover of the notebook your grandfather gave you. *Aude Volāre.* You wonder what the words mean. Turning the book over and over, you leaf through the pages, recognizing the looping script and realize your grandfather had scrawled a message. It reads,

**"Life's journey is not a destination, it's a dance in the tide—
so loosen up and enjoy the ride."**

The page of the notebook crackles slightly as you turn it. The familiar scent of old paper and stale coffee rises, a faded circular stain in the corner, just where your Grandfather Muse rested his mug.

Your grandfather was always scribbling something between philosophy and mischief. This time, it's not a story, but an invitation etched in black ink, with a faint, brown coffee ring in the corner.

"Two paths lie ahead," he writes,
"and both require a bit of courage."

Choice One

Travel north to the Upper Peninsula of Michigan, where Lake Superior rolls like an inland sea, and a stand-up paddleboard race becomes a lesson in rhythm, resilience and endurance.

FIND CHAPTER 1: MOVEMENT • PAGE 13

Choice Two

Start in Cobb County, Georgia, before stepping inside a Loire Valley castle in France, where the view from each window reshapes the way you see your own journey. Ready to climb the winding stairs and look at life from a higher vantage point?

FIND CHAPTER 2: PERSPECTIVE • PAGE 21

At the bottom of the page, in your grandfather's unmistakable scrawl, "Muse on this . . . remember, still water stagnates. Go where the current dares to take you."

A small, hand-drawn compass rose appears on the bottom corner of the page. The ink is smudged, but the lines are steady, pointing toward something more than north.

Riding the Current

PERSPECTIVE ALIGNED, MOVEMENT UNDERWAY

CHAPTER 1

Movement

*I'm having trouble grasping what my life will be like in the future . . .
I keep yelling at my inner self, "Where do I even start?"*
ERIONNA S.

**JUNE, WHITEFISH POINT
UPPER PENINSULA, MICHIGAN U.S.A.
46.8°N, 85.0°W**

It is an unusually warm June day, you are driving twelve hours north toward Lake Superior. Your beloved car is a loyal heap of ambition, odd noises, and one very bright check-engine light. The bumper sticker—*Honk if you love dairy farmers*—isn't your vibe, but she came with it.

You have signed up for a five-mile standup paddleboard race, known as SUP racing, as an excuse to return to this mighty waterfront. During the long road trip, you binged on french fries and podcasts. Approaching the water, you nearly choke on your overindulgence seeing a hundred colorful racers lined up on the rocky beach.

This Great Lake seems more like an ocean, lined with rare agate gemstones shining with red, orange, and yellow bands. You remember this shore from your childhood, where you ran up and down the sand dunes with your grandfather.

Unloading your board, nearly twelve-feet long with a paddle as tall as you are, your thoughts twist to follow the same pattern as the waves hitting the shore. You think about the competition. Can you stay on your board in this surf? Will you get sunburned? Have you eaten too many fries? Will you find a prized agate stone? Will you make new friends or maybe more? These thoughts rapid fire simultaneously through your brain.

The race sponsor, John, strides toward you. Looking deep into your eyes, he says, "I have some advice for you. Don't let competition distract you, and don't let the churned-up water rattle you. Keep your focus, and keep moving. Stay balanced. Don't paddle too fast, and don't paddle too slow. Consistency is the key. And mostly, just have fun!"

You whisper to yourself, "What was that about?" As you watch John strut through the coarse pebbles to the starting line and grab the whistle and bullhorn, you think, *That seems like a powerful punch of advice.*

With the sound of the whistle and John's words ringing in your ears, you shove your board into the water. With focused conviction, you block out the sounds of other racers. You stand upright on the spine of the board and dig your paddle into the churning waves. The surf is rough, but you stand firm and balanced.

Growing more confident with each stroke, you begin to paddle faster and faster. You laugh, realizing your wake could almost pull a water skier. Now, you're really going fast, but your inexperienced form pushes the nose of your board into the rushing water and you are nearly thrown overboard.

You regain balance but are now worried about staying ahead of the pack. Casting a quick glance behind you to measure your advantage over the others, you lean too hard on your right foot, and the nose of your board bursts out of the water. Your posture torques right and then left as you work hard to regain your balance. You nearly go under!

In response to this near disaster, you stop paddling, and once again the board begins to bob and shake. With the lack of movement, balance becomes an impossible task.

Only a mile into the race, you are reminded of John's important words. If you paddle too quickly, you can easily lose balance. You also note that if you paddle too slowly, you can easily lose balance.

. . .

Sometimes when we are in the middle of a change, or in an unfamiliar environment, we freeze out of fear and limit our movement, or contrastingly, we flail and convulse like we're drowning. Just like with the paddleboard, too much movement, or lack thereof, can cause us to lose our balance.

Nature gives us important clues.

Over time, I have learned to look to nature for rich principles that can help guide our actions.

Why is consistent movement important?

Ever seen stagnant water? The kind that just sits there, not a ripple in sight. That's the opposite of a serene pond, it's a five-star resort for mold.

Recently, I had the pleasure (and by pleasure, I mean trauma) of experiencing a sewer backup in my house. Let's not linger on that mental image. The cleanup crew's mission was clear: stop the black mold before it took up occupancy in my home.

At the same time, I was helping an elderly friend tidy her bathroom. I lifted her shower mat (innocently, mind you) and uncovered a thriving ecosystem. A full-on mold metropolis. Turns out, when water is trapped, it gets funky fast. Literally.

It's a fascinatingly gross topic, unless your aim is to become a microbiologist, in which case, I bet you're already taking notes.

But, keep in mind . . . the smallest movement in water breaks the surface tension and gives constructive life to the environment.

Even movement backwards doesn't stagnate . . . think about that for a moment!

The same holds true for us, even the smallest movement gives us meaning, purpose, vibrancy, and life. Maybe you've never had surgery, but if you have, you know doctors want you to move your body the same day as your operation. As John advised before the race, keep moving, not too fast or too slow.

This movement mantra can positively impact so many different areas of your life from your physical health to your professional wellbeing.

. . .

In the middle of the sweaty race, it dawns on you that John's advice about paddling is a good analogy for your own life too:

**stay focused, limit distractions, keep moving,
find balance, and remain consistent.**

Swoosh, swoosh, swoosh. Your long paddle begins artfully guiding your board in the right direction with a consistent cadence. A smile spreads across your face. "Now I'm having fun," you utter to yourself. After all, those were John's parting words. "Mostly, just have fun!"

With that revelation, Sia's hit song "Unstoppable" kicks in—*I'm a Porsche with no brakes.* You're not just ready to move—you're built to surge forward.

I'm unstoppable
I'm a Porsche with no brakes
I'm invincible . . .
I'm so confident
Yeah, I'm unstoppable today.

Crossing the finish line, despite your early mistakes, you are thrilled to see that you are among the top group of racers. You're ecstatic, especially since this is your first race. Most importantly, you are having fun and learning the importance of consistent movement. On the beach, bystanders give you high fives and you take a moment to soak in feelings of accomplishment and pride.

You find John and thank him for his astounding advice. You tell him that his words are more than just paddleboard insights; they are life advice! You dig for a pen and paper in your backpack and write down, "Keep focused. Limit distractions. Move consistently—not too fast, not too slow. Most importantly, have fun!"

Reminded of Grandfather Muse, you sketch a small compass rose in the bottom corner of the paper. You quietly fold the note and put it between the pages of your notebook, knowing this message will be important to your future.

PROPELLER PLAN Steps to Restore Movement

Movement is the heartbeat of every journey. Even the smallest shift in our daily rhythm can spark momentum that carries us toward new horizons. Before you chart your next course, pause to reflect on these points:

1. **Identify the Stagnant Space.** In what area of your life do you need more movement?

2. **Take the First Step.** How, and in what way, can you add small movements to that part of your life?

3. **Notice the Overdrive.** Is there an area of your life where you are moving too fast without aim or focus?

4. **Find Direction.** What would it look like to control that movement?

5. **Restore Focus.** In what ways could you regain focus in this area?

Clarity results when we choose our movements with care. Each thoughtful step, whether slowing down to regain focus or pushing forward with renewed energy, becomes part of your larger voyage. Let these points be your compass as you adjust your sails and move with purpose toward what matters most.

CHOOSE-YOUR-CURRENT

Once again, John—your ever-watchful paddleboard advisor—appears at the shoreline just as the sun begins its slow descent. But this time, he offers no lecture, no gentle course correction. Instead, he hands you a piece of paper; weather-worn and rippled with dried water drops, it reads:

*Two adventures lie ahead, if you're bold enough
to take the leap, benefits you'll reap.*

He tilts his head toward the horizon, in a nod to the journey ahead.

Choice One

Step into the glass-and-steel heights of a bustling brokerage firm in Atlanta, Georgia, where the view is dazzling, the pace relentless, and the winds at the top can shift without warning.

FIND CHAPTER 3: SETBACKS • PAGE 31

Choice Two

Shadow a champion athlete in the snowy birch-lined trails of Norway, discovering that the slip of a ski can teach more than the smoothest run.

FIND CHAPTER 4: MISTAKES • PAGE 41

John says, "It's your decision—but don't forget: the best journeys come with sand in your shoes and wind in your hair." Before vanishing into the choppy surf, John hands you a beautiful agate stone. The breeze shifts, and you feel a quiet pull toward the unknown.

CHAPTER 2

Perspective

How do you navigate from the point when you are in limbo; not knowing what will happen next? We're scared of not knowing what's coming next.
LAILA H.

**JULY, COBB GALLERIA
MARIETTA, GEORGIA U.S.A.
34.0°N, 84.5°W**

It is a smoldering July day and you are in the parking lot of the trendy casual restaurant where you took a job waiting tables after graduating until you can find what you believe to be a "real job." You want more fun and adventure, but you can barely pay rent as it is for your tiny, shared apartment. Your apartment complex is named Stoneridge, but you think it's more accurately called Stoned-ridge.

The amount of money you make during the slow lunch shift doesn't even come close to covering your third of the rent. Frankly, it won't even buy your lunch.

You squint against the bright rays of sun, a stark contrast to the dim restaurant. In the light of day, you grapple with the fact you need to cancel your evening plans and take on the dinner shift too. Stalking back into the restaurant, you ask if you can work a "double." The manager eyes your dirty uniform but agrees because another employee is sick. You are relieved and angry at the same time. Exhaustion overtakes you at the close of your shift. You detest the sauce stains running from your hair to your fingernails, but at least you are closer to making rent.

As you think about your job waiting tables, you know deep down it's not where you want to be long term. You're ready for a change, but the uncertainty of where to start makes moving forward a challenge.

. . .

Making progress can feel overwhelming, and often we become complacent burying ourselves in distractions and the daily grind.

"I don't know, I don't know" rings repeatedly in our ears. We listen to the uncertainty and give it roots to grow bigger and gnarlier.

"All senior year of college, everyone asks, *what's next?*
or *any job offers?* Although probably asked in good nature,
this can be overwhelming to someone who has spent the
last twelve to fourteen consecutive years of their life in school.
To have a norm taken from you is scary."

ALIVIA

We ask ourselves, "What do I do if I don't know what to do? Where do I begin?" The answers to these questions are NOT simple; they require many small, but significant, steps to get to an answer. Sometimes we stumble, other times we fall, but the important part is to keep taking small steps . . . and get perspective.

Perspective is vital! You can't see a picture if you are standing too close or staring at it for too long.

Take a step back, give it distance and time, and revisit it with the space to see the whole picture with fresh eyes.

My mother is a professional portrait artist. One of her key pieces of advice is, "Get perspective." During her painting process she moves to stand several paces from the canvas to obtain a new vantage point. She even uses a mirror to view the painting backward, a magnifying glass to amplify her strokes, or turns the canvas upside down. With these small actions she can see things otherwise missed.

Myopia, when close objects look clear but far objects look blurry, is an artist's kryptonite and can seriously weaken their creative output.

In the same way, when we are too close to our own lives, we are unable to clearly see the way forward. The best defense against myopia is to stand back and get perspective.

• • •

The chaos and lack of clear direction in your own life leads you down an online rabbit hole. Searching for your next opportunity, you stop scrolling when you see a study abroad program in France. You smile at the possibility and note it's the first time you've smiled in awhile. You certainly don't have the money to go to France, but there's a strong urge pulling you in that direction.

Several days later you're still plotting ways to make this trip happen, and you even talk to the professor and your family about next steps. With that, you set the necessary actions into motion, planning ways to save money, digging deep into your pockets, and resorting to student loans to fund the rest.

Now, one year later on another July day, instead of finding yourself in the parking lot of the trendy casual restaurant, your feet are now planted on foreign soil. The experience is simultaneously difficult and thrilling. In a burst of adventure and impulse, you buy a Eurorail Train Pass, and with a ragged backpack and a dream, you bravely leave Paris for the famed Loire Valley on the western side of France.

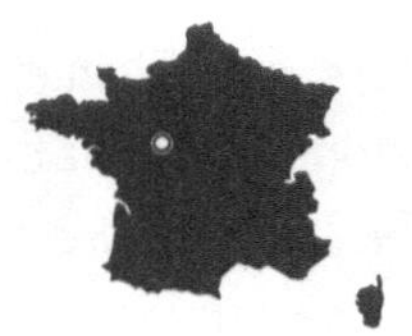

JULY, RANDOM MEDIEVAL CASTLE
LOIRE VALLEY, FRANCE
47.6°N, 1.0°E

At the station waiting for your rail adventure, you sit on a bench tagged by layers of graffiti. Perched quietly, you are taken by the image of a one-legged pigeon awkwardly hobbling to eat trash at the passengers' feet. This image stuns and haunts you.

Once tucked in your seat on the train, you search your phone and discover that pigeons can fly up to 90 miles per hour and travel very long distances over several days at a time. The one-legged bird you saw had healthy, striped wings and you wondered why it didn't fly to a nearby park with tasty food, clean water, and a pastoral setting instead of picking at trash in the noisy train station.

Looking out the window at the passing yellow fields, you muse, *Is it possible I have been living like the one-legged pigeon; hopping around, eating trash, rather than flying to my potential? Maybe, just maybe, this trip is needed to understand what it is like to fly.*

The train squeals to a stop at a village with a hyphenated name you can't pronounce. Observing a medieval castle in the distance, you believe it's a perfect place to explore. Impulsively, you grab your bag and leap out the door, onto the platform, and to your next quest.

It's a Monday and you realize your plans are thwarted, finding the castle dark, every port closed. Tracing the exterior, the pea stone crunches beneath your boots, the walls beckon you, making you wishful for access. Then, a wave of chills runs down your neck and arms when you see the profile of a gardener, who for an instant looks like your Grandfather Muse in his yellow sun hat and green pants.

The gardener is the only other person on the property, and he draws toward the towering front gate. Whistling a familiar tune, he pulls a skeleton key out of his pocket and opens the wooden door as if breaking a treasured seal. With the gesture of his hand, the gardener invites you to explore, and you find yourself alone among the ancient walls.

Without thought, your feet take you one step forward and another step forward down a long stone corridor, the sun peeking through the beveled glass soaring skyward. Gasping, you hold your breath reverently. Silence. The wrinkled time plays tricks on your eyes. You listen intently, ready for spirits of the past to offer sound advice.

Emotions fill you from feet up, and the tension between what you are and what you could be is palpable.

An invisible cape appears on your shoulders and drapes to the ground, evoking a regal confidence. Your movements are measured. Your gait is graceful, your posture straight. You ask yourself if this could be the feeling of royalty, of belonging?

At the end of the long hall, there is a winding stone stairway. You hoist your invisible robe and take one step after another up the time-worn flight of stairs. This secret shaft leads to a cylindrical turret perched atop the roofline. The daredevil in your ear urges you to sit on the balcony with your feet over the dizzying edge.

You are surprised to see the Loire River snaking through the silver green distant hills. Osprey and European Honey Buzzards, practically at kissing distance, are circling at the same altitude as your soaring thoughts. Your feet feel free swinging against the stone wall as if your puppet strings have been cut.

After hours of basking on the transformative stone, you are struck with resolve. You've given yourself the space to stand back. Perched on the vista, you are pulled out of your myopic haze.

Once depressed, directionless, and despondent, you now feel

refreshed and motivated with a glimmer of possibility. At first you don't understand why the moment alone in the castle is so important. Your critical inner self says, *What's the big deal? You are just touring a building.*

But, as you leave the medieval castle, the gardener rounds the corner of the secret garden and walks toward you. He removes his yellow hat and eagerly hands you a crumpled note.

You look at the gardener inquisitively, eyes locked while carefully unfolding the note. Surprisingly, it is written in English and reads,

"Perspective is vital for seeing the big picture."

You internalize the message once more, soaking in the point-of-view from this definitive moment. You freeze when you see a hand drawn compass rose at the bottom of the paper, as if the gardener has channeled your Grandfather Muse. Deep in thought, you fold the note and reach into your backpack for your treasured notebook. Tucking the paper between two pages, you are quite sure you will want to reference this message again in the future.

PROPELLER PLAN The Gift of Perspective

A "perspective exercise" doesn't take long but the impact could be significant. For gaining a new perspective, stand back and consider from an overall macro lens three basic, but important, points:

1. **Shift from Limitation to Possibility.** Ask, "What CAN I do?" (Instead of looking at the closed opportunities or asking what you can't do.)

2. **Recognize your Present Strengths.** What unique capabilities do I have right now?

3. **Align Your Gifts with the Need.** What, where, or who needs what I can offer?

The answers to these questions may not come quickly, but take some time to consider them, and write down your answers as they come to you.

No matter how busy you are, take a few moments (as often as you can) to step away from your routine. It doesn't have to be to a foreign land, but take a break and press "F5 Refresh" on your life. Go to a park, a coffee shop, an art museum, the forest, a patch of garden, or anywhere that doesn't look like your daily surroundings.

Perspective often takes time. Plan it, set a date and location. In fact, set recurring dates. You'll be glad you did.

If you can't get away because you are a parent of small children or a caregiver, find a fresh place to sit in your home after everyone goes to bed. Face a chair in a different direction, hang upside down off your couch, put your head out the window, or lie down on the kitchen floor. Kids find new movements all the time. Why can't we adults?

In fact, I once had a manager ask the waitstaff at a restaurant to sit in new locations before each shift to view the eatery from a different angle. This allowed us to make necessary improvements to the environment if needed. This exercise on perspective is asking you to do the same and is crucial for clearly viewing your present state from a different angle.

There seems to be so much pressure to go, do, obtain, and gain, that it becomes easy to overlook what would actually help us grow in an authentic way that aligns with our purpose. (At our frenetic pace, we often don't even know what brings us meaning). It is invaluable to take thoughtful moments to breathe, think, and tap into the quiet direction that a fresh perspective can offer.

CHOOSE·YOUR·CURRENT

Back at the Loire Valley Château, beyond an ivy-laced archway, the gardener calls out to you once again. He wipes his brow, exhales with a grin, and says in his thick French accent: "I have an adventure for you—one that begins not in the garden, but in the wilds of ambition."

He gestures with a dirt-streaked hand toward two diverging horizons:

Choice One

Strap on your skis and follow a legendary Birkebeiner racer into snow-laced wilderness, where wiping out becomes the teacher, and every fall whispers its own wisdom.

FIND CHAPTER 4: MISTAKES · PAGE 41

Choice Two

Under a full moon, join the ropes in a Hawaiian midnight regatta, where you grasp that sailing's deepest lesson is resilience, the strength to free yourself from being in a rut.

FIND CHAPTER 5: STUCK · PAGE 49

As the gardener vanishes down the rose-lined path, he calls back with a wave and a wink, "Amuse-toi bien!" A phrase that lingers in the breeze—"have fun"—equal parts blessing and a dare.

⚓

SECTION III

Stormy Seas

WEATHERING
SETBACKS AND
SELF-DOUBT

CHAPTER 3

Setbacks

*How do you stay motivated to keep moving forward
during setbacks and challenges?*
YURI M.

**AUGUST, ATLANTA FINANCIAL CENTER
ATLANTA, GEORGIA U.S.A.
33.8°N, 84.4°W**

A recruiter looks you squarely in the eyes and says, "You would be perfect for a position at a brokerage firm." You try not to furrow your brow because brokerage firms are an enigma to you. You are, however, looking for purpose and progress . . . and money. You think perhaps a brokerage firm can fill all these needs for you. Besides, your empty wallet demands that you agree to the meeting.

The job interview takes place in an all-glass skyscraper in the heart of the financial and shopping district in Atlanta. The polished floors and private dining rooms are something you have only seen in movies. When the heavily paneled doors open to the trading floor, a high-tech room appears, flanked by large screen displays like a massive digital poker game.

Voices yell in staccato tempo to "buy!," "sell!," "buy!," "sell!"

The energy and excitement make you feel high. Four financial brokers with slick hair and cuff links hire you on the spot for their international department.

You are relieved and thrilled. You landed a "real job!"

"Whatever that means," you question to yourself.

On your first day, you're among the first to arrive. Your desk chair cradles your potential, and the cacophony of sounds you heard before is now deadened by the pre-dawn hours before the stock market opens. Documents are scattered around like leaves in a forest, written in a foreign language akin to hieroglyphics.

Your heartbeat echoes loudly, "What am I doing here?"

A parade of "haute couture" brand labels passes your desk as employees arrive to surf the market's waves. You are left alone and feeling painfully awkward.

It doesn't take long to realize you are working for four savage beasts; their fangs and gums exposed as they roar impossible commands at an unreasonable clip. Their words slice and dice you as if you were flesh on a cutting board. You never knew such degrading language was possible. Your self-esteem is battered and wounded enduring blow after blow.

You wince when you discover the international team's nickname is "the greed brothers;" it seems fitting. Conflicted between needing the job, but feeling life is too short to be treated so horribly, you are grossly disenchanted that your "real job" is turning into a real nightmare.

During your third week you are hit by an especially degrading attack, something about *shit for brains,* and you are overcome by the hot anger throbbing in your head. A display of weakness would be mortifying and the end of your short-lived career.

Having no idea where you are going, you escape down the nearest marble stairway and land squarely in the Chief Executive's office suite framed in leather and gold. You are like a mouse running from a feral cat and now find yourself nearing the mouth of the lion.

At this point, controlling your emotions is nearly impossible; then you hear the click-clack of high heels entering the corridor. Ashamed and exposed, as if stark naked, you step into a lush embankment of plants that flank the entrance to the suite.

A voice says your name, followed by, "Why are you hiding?"

Turning your head slightly, squinting, you see the Senior Vice President of Human Resources.

With a cracking voice, you whisper "I'm giving my two weeks' notice." She responds with, "Come into my office." (more like the lion's den.)

Sitting at the priceless antique table in an intimidating circle of prestige and power, are the President, Executive Vice President, and two Human Resource professionals. All eyes are on you, and it is nearly impossible to hide your terror when they tell you to take a seat in the leather wingback chair, a bit too close for comfort.

Vulnerability expresses itself as vertigo.

The President gives you his cloth handkerchief to dry your face. Now, you are completely mortified! It is impossible to remember why you originally wanted this job so badly.

One of the women from HR places her fingertips together and slowly says, "Tell us everything."

This is your moment to be professional, yet authentic. Although you have no intention of disclosing the stories of degrading treatment you've endured; you want out before the figurative riptide tows you underwater. Your thoughts are whirring so quickly in your head that the garble of conversation happening around you is unintelligible.

One of the executives draws a deep breath and hesitantly recounts the recent nearby shooting at another brokerage firm where nine people were killed and thirteen others injured.

The executive looks at you and firmly says, "You need to take a few days off for your own personal safety."

"What?" you exclaim. "My personal safety?" Before you can think, the words are spilling out of your mouth.

Your thoughts jumble like a tumbler of dice in your head. This is a serious setback and once again you choke back anger!

. . .

Fozzie is a jazz drummer and part-time philosopher whom I met when I lived close to the Atlanta Beltline, a twenty-two-mile walking trail loop where he often performs. One day, Fozzie saw me from a short distance and asked me why I looked so blue. I responded that I felt like I was taking too many steps backward in life.

Fozzie reminded me that we can't always move forward, sometimes backward movement is necessary. He then gave the example of a baseball pitcher. They pull their arm backward to propel the ball forward. Fozzie mimicked the movement with his right arm as the invisible ball went sailing.

He looked at me with glistening eyes to make sure I got the message. I did! What a powerful image.

Sometimes you must move backward to move forward.

For a moment, you consider how nature provides similar examples: ocean waves ebb backward and flow forward; vines curl in on themselves first to anchor and then climb higher; pruning is the act of cutting back trees to allow for fuller and stronger new growth; even caterpillars inch backward before pushing onward.

If you take a few minutes, you can probably think of stinging setbacks in your own life. Setbacks are a reality of every journey, but believe it or not, when a situation seems like a setback, it could be setting the scene for a leap forward.

Sometimes we must first go backward to move forward.

When you are in what seems like backward movement, think about the possibility that it could be a countdown for the launch forward. To punctuate this point, there are many famous setback stories.

Tori Murden McClure

Tori Murden McClure, whom I met one time, was the first woman and first American to row solo across the Atlantic Ocean. The first time she attempted the feat in 1998, she was derailed by a massive hurricane, nearly killed, and had to be rescued by a crew on a freightliner. Later that year she met Muhammad Ali, the famed heavyweight boxer, and he said to her, "Do you want to be known as the woman who ALMOST rowed across the Atlantic Ocean?" This gave Tori the spark she needed, and she completed the solo-crossing in 1999. [1]

Walt Disney

Walt Disney was fired for "lacking imagination" and went bankrupt before founding his Magic Kingdom. When he died in 1966, Disney's net worth was between $100 to $150 million, or $1 billion in current dollars. [2]

Emma "Grandma" Gatewood

Emma "Grandma" Gatewood was sixty-seven years old when she became the first woman to solo hike the entire 2,190-mile Appalachian Trail in one season in 1955. Just a year earlier, she attempted the journey but broke her only pair of glasses and wore out shoes that were never meant for hiking. With renewed resolve, she returned home to better prepare and then started once again to finally conquer the feat. [3]

Steven Spielberg

Steven Spielberg was rejected by film school three times. Yet, he has directed thirty-two feature films, won three Academy Awards, four Golden Globe Awards, two BAFTA Awards, as well as the AFI Life Achievement Award. [4]

Oprah Winfrey

Oprah Winfrey was fired from her first job as a news anchor and demoted from a primetime co-anchor role. Undeterred, she started her own television show and network media company. She now has a net worth of $3.1 billion.[5]

Charles Schulz

Charles Schulz, the creator of the Peanuts cartoons, was rejected from Central High School's yearbook staff in St. Paul, Minnesota, and turned down for a job at Walt Disney Studios. The Peanuts comic strip ran for fifty years, had forty-four TV specials, and was the most popular and influential comic strip of all time. [6]

Michael Jordan

Michael Jordan was cut from the Laney High School varsity basketball team in Wilmington, North Carolina because his coach didn't think he was tall enough. Now, at 6 feet 6 inches, he's considered the greatest basketball player of all time with a net worth of $3.5 billion.[7]

Diana Nyad

Diana Nyad attempted the "impossible" swim from Cuba to Florida four times before she successfully completed the swim on her fifth attempt at age sixty-four, becoming the first person to do so unassisted without a shark cage. She is known for saying, "Never, ever give up!" [8]

• • •

Back at the highly polished executive table, you are told to take a few days off for your personal safety.

You find yourself stuttering, "My . . . my personal safety?"

The president continues calmly, "When you return, we will transfer you to the Soft Dollar department."

In a swirl of confusion, you have no idea what Soft Dollar is or what the department does, but you find yourself nodding at his offer.

This offer becomes a foothold, the foothold becomes a promotion, the promotion becomes the opportunity to start a business, and so goes the movement of one step back, two steps forward.

Ten years later, at a local restaurant you see the same president who turned your setback into a leap forward.

With a pleased look on his face, he says to you, "Do you remember the day when you met with the executives about your transition at the firm?"

Your gut churns, how could you forget?

He tells you that they insisted on maintaining your employment and transferring you to another division because of your incredible work ethic and positive attitude.

The President finishes the conversation saying, "You were exactly the type of person we wanted at the firm, and we were better off because you were there."

Just before leaving, he shakes your hand and places a folded note in your palm.

As he walks away, you ponder his message knowing you'll never forget it. You unfold the note and read it slowly. It says,

**"Sometimes backward movement leads to forward motion . . .
and don't worry about returning my handkerchief,
I don't need it back."**

You laugh to yourself remembering that definitive day when you mopped your face at the antique table of intimidation. You refold the piece of paper, and place it between two pages of your trusted notebook. This is a meeting you will never forget.

PROPELLER PLAN Setbacks as Starting Points for Growth

Just as a rough tide knocks you around, sometimes the very storm that batters you is the one that carries you to new waters.

Trust that setbacks can facilitate growth when you hold steady and keep moving forward.

Think back to a time when a setback forced you in an unexpected direction that ultimately turned out better. Write down:

1. **Acknowledge the Hurt.** What felt painful or unfair in that moment?

2. **Discover the Hidden Gain.** What new opportunity, strength, or insight came because of it?

3. **Transform Pain into Perspective.** How can you apply that same perspective the next time you face a setback?

This reflection turns hindsight into foresight and equips you to face your next challenge with resilience and clarity.

CHOOSE-YOUR-CURRENT

The former President steps back through the restaurant door, eyes gleaming like someone who's emerged from the storm. He leans close and says with a half-smile,

"Adventure is knocking. This is your moment."
He gestures to two paths, each shimmering like a mirage.

Choice One

Travel with a trusted friend to Scotland and the edge of the North Sea, where mist carries the courage to speak your truth.

FIND CHAPTER 6: THE VALUE OF YOUR VOICE • PAGE 59

Choice Two

Find refuge in an ancient family homestead tucked into the foot-hills of Algeria, where quiet becomes your guide and you learn the ease of being your authentic self.

FIND CHAPTER 7: WELL IN YOUR SKIN • PAGE 69

Before the president disappears into the night, he turns back once more and says in a low voice, "Setbacks are sly things . . . they're often just courage in disguise."

CHAPTER 4

Mistakes

A professional career in the field you study is nerve racking.
I found myself trying to apply to easy jobs that felt comfortable
and avoiding the ones in my field.

MELANIE Z.

JANUARY, BIRKEBEINER SKI TRAIL
LILLEHAMMER, NORWAY
61.1°N, 10.5° E

The temperature is -23 degrees Fahrenheit and the windchill tugs at the gauge until it is an astounding 75 degrees BELOW zero. You are wrapped head to toe in thick ski gear to protect yourself from frostbite. In southeastern Norway, two hours north of the capital Oslo, the terrain is undulating and hillier than you expected.

As a kid, you thought cross-country skiing was easy. Of course it was, you had no clue how good you had it on the beginner trails. Now, you're braving the inhospitable cold to practice with an instructor in preparation for the Birkebeiner, a cross-country ski race as intense as its name. You can barely pronounce it, let alone imagine finishing it.

Swooshing sounds beneath your skis as you graze across the

groomed corduroy path. (Yes, that's what it's really called.) It has been a decade since you last put on your skis and your knees are stiff. You are more terrified of falling than you expected. Your gait looks more akin to that of the tinman from *The Wizard of Oz.*

Ingrid, your sage instructor, has competed thirty-five times through the thick pine forests of the Nordic ski marathon. She knows every up and down of the undulating snow-covered hills, and you are sure her veteran advice is just what you need. She laughs as she tells you about the time her ski broke during one race and she had to hobble to the finish line.

Ingrid barks orders and guides you toward an especially steep upward climb. You didn't even know it was possible to ski uphill to this sharp degree, but with Ingrid by your side, she teaches you the correct stance. The wind blows diagonally with jagged jaws, and you set your teeth against this chilling challenge. Figuratively shifting to low gear, you widen your stance and point your toes outward.

Shoop, shoop, shoop . . . plop! You fall, face-planting into the icy snow, utterly embarrassed.

"How can you fall going uphill?" you shout above the gale force wind.

Ingrid stops and quips, "Good for you. It's obvious you're trying hard." She continues, "If you don't fall, you aren't trying hard enough."

Digesting what she just said, you unscramble your skis and stand up, albeit with stiff knees and a sustained fear of falling.

Ingrid stops you, finds your eyes through the ski gear and says, "Crashes occur, poles are broken. Just give yourself grace and start slowly." Then she challenges, "For every time you fall, I will add five Norwegian Krone to a gift card to Lillehammer Sport Shop. Do we have a deal?"

"Mistakes are necessary and stumbles are normal. Progress NOT perfection is what we should ask of ourselves."

"Deal!" you reply.

. . .

"To live a creative life, we must lose our fear of being wrong."
JOSEPH CHILTON PEARCE

"8% of people on average are okay with mistakes. 92% see a mistake as bad and, ideally, try to avoid it." [9]

Each semester I teach 275 sales and marketing students, and I require them to make presentations both virtually and in person. Effective, articulate speaking is one of the most powerful skills one can develop. Yet it's striking to me how often students punish themselves for a perceived "mess up," dropping their heads, shuffling their feet, or even fighting back tears. Many of these students have never given a presentation in front of an audience, so naturally, they are going to make mistakes. That's where growth begins.

I come from a family who took perfectionism to the next level. My father mowed the lawn in a suit and dress-shoes, we relentlessly picked lint off the carpet, and I ran screaming out of history class in high school when I got a B+ on a quiz.

The pièce de résistance was when my sister and I brought butane curling irons on a flight so we could style our hair mid-air and land looking perfect (how airlines ever allowed flammables onboard is another story).

Finally, while in graduate school, a decade into my career, I tried to give up the notion that I needed to be perfect. Literally crying, I told my sister that I couldn't keep up with school and work full-time. The load was crushing me.

My sister gave me some sage advice, "You only need to jump through the hoops. You don't need to polish the hoops before jumping through them."

Those words felt as foreign to my ears as they did to her mouth. Accepting your shortcomings, and the shortcomings of others, is the first step to recovering from perfectionism. Recovery isn't about lowering your standards; it's about releasing the grip of impossible ones. It means giving yourself permission to learn out loud, to stumble forward, and to see mistakes as stepping stones, not verdicts. True progress comes not from flawless execution, but from resilience, adaptability, and the courage to try again.

> *"There will be many times when we won't look good to ourselves or anyone else. We need to stop demanding that we do. It is impossible to get better and look good at the same time."*
> **THE ARTIST WAY**

There are three striking stories of famous individuals and their insights about mistakes and perfection:

Yo-Yo Ma

Yo-Yo Ma was a child musical prodigy and is the world's most well-known cellist. He has recorded ninety-two albums and received nineteen Grammy Awards. He has been a United Nations Messenger of Peace since 2006, received the National Medal of Arts in 2001, and the Presidential Medal of Freedom in 2011. Yo-Yo Ma was named one of Time Magazine's 100 Most Influential People of 2020.

In Ma's Masterclass he aims to create magical experiences. He remembers, "At one point I had the audacity to think I could play a perfect concert ... and I was bored out of my mind. That was the moment I made a fateful decision that I was actually going to devote my life to human expression versus human perfection." [10]

Find the beauty of playing in the realm of human expression versus human perfection.

Julia Child

Julia Child was an acclaimed American chef, author, and television personality who was recognized for having brought French cuisine to the American public. She wrote Mastering the Art of French Cooking, *and in 1963 debuted the television cooking show* The French Chef.

When Julia first tasted French food, she said, "[It was] an opening up of the soul and spirit for me." She graduated from the famous Cordon Bleu cooking school in Paris. Her kitchen, designed by her husband, was the backdrop for three of her television shows and is on display at the Smithsonian National Museum of American History. Interestingly, Julia Child did not discover her passion for cooking until the age of thirty-seven! (A testament that passion can be found at any age!)

There is a famous television episode of Julia making a potato dish. She tried to flip the pressed cake of fried potatoes on live television and half of it went sliding onto the stovetop. The talk track from the episode records:

"I'm going to try (to flip) it anyway.
You must have the courage of your convictions . . .
(after the potatoes fall) ah, that didn't go very well.
I didn't have the courage to do it the way I should have,
but you can always pick it up.
The only way you learn to do things, is just to do it.
You haven't lost anything, and you can always turn it
into something else." [11]

Amanda Anisimova

Organized by the All England Lawn Tennis and Croquet Club since 1877, Wimbledon is the oldest and most widely regarded tennis tournament in the world. During the 2025 tournament, the 23-year-old American, Amanda Anisimova made it to the women's singles finals competing head-to-head with Iga Swiatek from Poland.

Anisimova lost a painful 6-0, twice! It was claimed to be "the most one-sided loss in 114 years."

This is where the story gets interesting. It took five minutes and a few tears for Anisimova to reframe her failure into something totally different. She graciously complimented her opponent, thanked the fans, and courageously confessed, "I know I didn't have enough today, but I'm going to keep putting in the work. I always believe in myself, so I hope to be back here (at Wimbledon) again one day." [12]

Can you believe how open, honest, vulnerable, and generous she was after the most devastating failure in the sport of tennis? Consider that lesson in other areas of life.

The best people, (athletes, artists, companies) fail more, NOT less. The most successful and high-performing people are the ones who accept their mistakes, but choose to correct their choices, their path, and their trajectory. Anisimova reframed her loss as an opportunity for growth.

Author Marianne Williamson said it best, "Pain can burn you up and destroy you, or burn you up and redeem you."

. . .

At the Lillehammer Sport Shop, you run your hand along the racks of warm ski jackets. The fabric balances form and comfort, resilient yet inviting, much like this experience. You pat your pocket, touching the gift card from Ingrid, your encouraging ski instructor who rewarded you for every dramatic fall.

At checkout, you retrieve the card to pay but discover something tucked behind it: a folded note, scribbled on the back of a flyer for the upcoming Birkebeiner race.

Etched across the page in block print, Ingrid reminds you:

**"It pays to make mistakes, don't dodge them, lean in.
You will be better off for it**." It ends with kindness and confidence:
"We'll see you at the finish line. You've got this."

PROPELLER PLAN *Learning from Mistakes*

Mistakes aren't evidence of failure; they're proof you were brave enough to try. Every misstep is a marker on the map, showing you where the rocks are and teaching you how to steer more skillfully next time. Instead of dragging you under, mistakes can be the very waves that lift you higher if you choose to ride them with resilience! Think of one recent mistake, big or small, that still lingers in your mind. Write down:

1. Find the Lesson Beneath the Misstep. What have you learned from that mistake?

2. Recognize Growth in the Aftermath. How did you, or could you, grow because of it?

3. Let the Lesson Guide Your Next Step. How will you apply that lesson moving forward?

Then reframe it in your reflection: replace the word "mistake" with "lesson." This simple shift serves to remind you that past errors don't define you, but make the future YOU better and wiser.

CHOOSE-YOUR-CURRENT

You step outside the Nordic ski shop with a new jacket and a softened spirit. The wind still bites, but it doesn't seem as sharp now. Warmth blooms from somewhere within.

Back in the car, you glance again at the note from Ingrid, this time flipping it over. A message is waiting, inked on the printed flyer in a different hand:

**"You've found your pace and now, you're not afraid to fall.
An adventure awaits, if you're willing to follow the call."**

Choice One

Board a flight to Scotland with an old friend, winding along the rugged coast where you will learn that voice isn't found, it's claimed.

FIND CHAPTER 6: THE VALUE OF YOUR VOICE • PAGE 59

Choice Two

Journey into the pulse of India, where rickshaws weave through crowded streets and temple bells echo above the din. Amidst the swirl of color and sound, you find yourself before a guide whose wisdom cuts through the chaos.

FIND CHAPTER 8: GOOD THING, BAD THING • PAGE 77

At the bottom corner, faint but unmistakable: a compass rose, encircled by the smudge of a coffee ring.

You smile. Grandfather Muse has clearly been here, too.

CHAPTER 5

Stuck

MAY, THE MOKES
KAILUA BEACH, HAWAII U.S.A.
21.4°N, 157.7°W

The inky black darkness surrounds Magic, your thirty-two-foot sailboat, to the point you can hardly see the silhouettes of the palm-fringed shoreline of Kailua Beach on the windward side of O'ahu. It's a calm May night, and you and your new fellow sailor friends are competing in a midnight sailing regatta against two dozen other boats. You met the gregarious captain, with a likeness to Santa Claus, and his crew at a beach front tiki hut, and you couldn't resist the offer to participate in the late-night race.

The light of the full moon is dulled by an eerie cloud cover that plays tricks on your eyes. After a whirlwind lesson, you learn to fly the spinnaker, the large colorful sail at the front of the boat that captures wind coming from behind. Your boat bobs up and down, challenging your coordination and balance. The phrase "getting your sea legs" has taken on a new meaning for you.

Holding the ropes in your gloved hands, you recount that you took this impromptu trip to Hawaii because you found a discount flight that made the cross-continent trip enticing. After all, your heartbeat chants, *you only live once.*

Standing behind the pulpit, near the bow of the boat, you notice the beauty of the evening despite the darkness. The temperature is perfect, and there is no sound except for the gentle lap of water against the hull of the vessel. You can't wait to tell your friends about this incredibly peaceful moment.

Suddenly, WHAM! CRACK! CREAK!

Your feet kick into the air and the ropes tear from your hands. Your spine crashes one vertebra at a time onto the deck of the boat. There is a dissonant chorus of shrieks from both the boat and its crew!

Then silence . . . your boat hits rock! And then mud!

Your keel, the bottom fin of the boat, has caught the shallows of the basaltic volcano, known as "The Mokes" twin islets (pronounced with a long 'o' like yolk).

You went from sailing full speed ahead to completely grounded in a split second. You learn the term for being stuck in a boat is "running aground."

You are stuck. In the dark. No tugboat around.

• • •

Sir Ernest Shackleton

Sir Ernest Shackleton was caught in a similar situation.[13] *His boat was also stuck, but his circumstances were far more extraordinary.*

The year was 1914. Shackleton, his crew of twenty-seven men, sixty-nine sled dogs, and one cat were aboard the HMS Endurance. They left London, England with the goal of crossing the Antarctic continent via the South Pole: known as the Imperial Trans-Antarctic Expedition.

The crew successfully sailed to South Georgia Island located half-way between Argentina and Antarctica. Two days after leaving the island they encountered pack ice and spent five weeks battling its frozen claws. Suddenly the ship became trapped, and they could no longer sail forward. They were stranded!

Endurance and her crew were trapped for approximately nine months before the ship was eventually crushed by the ice and sank! Can you imagine the horror?

The men were forced to flee the ship and set up camp on the surrounding ice floe, which they aptly named, Patience Camp. The environment of living on a chunk of ice was inhumane. CONTENT ADVISORY: the only food they had to eat was their sled dogs, penguins, and seals. The average temperatures fluctuated between -4 to -35 degrees Fahrenheit! That's nearly 70 degrees below freezing, not accounting for windchill!

Get this! The Endurance crew was stranded on ice for a total of 20 months! That's nearly two years in the frigid, barren terrain with no real shelter or protection and no real hope of rescue. Even more impressive, NOT one person died. Not one! That's incredible.

> *"How do you stay motivated and confident when [life]*
> *doesn't give you exactly what you hoped for?"*
> **ELIZABETH L.**

How did Shackleton and his crew manage to stay alive for nearly two years under the most dire circumstances? Certainly, this experience was not what they had hoped for. In my opinion, they stayed alive because they continued to engage in daily activities despite their extraordinary circumstances.

Under Shackleton's incredible leadership, the crew developed a rigorous regimen of daily activities, which included chores such as cleaning, hunting, building, mending, and cooking. In addition to their work, they made time in their routine for games, joke telling, singing, banjo playing, photography, scientific studies, socializing, and camaraderie.

They also kept log recordings, today's version of a diary, of all activities and details about their location and environment.

All while stranded on ice.

Can you imagine taking the time for games and singing amidst such a potentially deadly situation? Routine, purpose, community, humor, and joy gave this stranded crew a mental, and eventually a physical, lifeline.

On August 30, 1916, after being stuck for 608 days, all twenty-eight men were safely rescued!

. . .

Your small sailboat hitting The Mokes during midrace isn't nearly as dramatic as the Endurance mission, but it certainly feels frightening, especially in the pitch dark. Your captain gives each of you a specific role to help dislodge the vessel from the volcanic rock. One crew member sets the sail to help the wind pull the boat off from the entrapment. You and another mate jump overboard into the dark waters to push the stubborn wreck (you try hard not to imagine creatures slithering around your toes), and the captain guides the way from behind the helm.

When a boat runs aground, like Magic did off the coast of Hawaii, it is easy to feel paralyzed by the weight of stillness. Progress halts, fear creeps in, and the temptation to despair looms large, especially in darkness! Yet Shackleton's crew reminds us that being "stuck" is not the end of the journey, it is often the point where resilience is forged. Survival is not built on flawless circumstances, but on how you show up and look for creative solutions when movement seems impossible.

PROPELLER PLAN Getting Unstuck

Steps to take when you feel stuck:

1. Anchor with Purpose. Sometimes when you're stuck, your ultimate "why" may feel elusive or uncertain. In these moments, shrink the horizon; find purpose in the little things. Take one step at a time; engage in a simple routine, or even make a commitment to show up for others.

2. Take Small Steps. In your own stuck moments, break the situation into bite-sized chunks. Take small steps: send the email, organize your space, check in with a colleague. Progress doesn't always roar; sometimes it tiptoes . . . and those small steps, when multiplied, can shift your entire course.

3. Fuel Up While You Wait. When you feel stuck, despair can threaten to sink your spirits. Don't underestimate the power of including music, games, and humor into your routine.

Joy is not frivolous; it is survival!

When you're mired in stillness, joy and laughter might feel impossible, but you don't need to host a grand celebration. Ask yourself, what actions can you schedule that bring you joy? These could include: watching funny videos, playing a game of hoops, calling a friend who makes you laugh, or listening to live music. This list is different for everyone, but the point is being intentional about creating a routine that makes time for moments of joy.

When you feel immobile, remember this survival playbook. Even small acts can become lifeboats that carry you through the waiting, keeping despair at bay until momentum returns. You can endure the seemingly impossible, not because you are free from hardship, but because you have learned to cling fiercely to meaning, contribution, and connection . . . until the ice finally cracks.

~~~~

CHOOSE-YOUR-CURRENT

When Magic is finally securely tied in her slip and the ropes are stowed, Captain Claus unzips his duffle bag and hands you a crumpled note. The ruddy captain clasps your hand in a firm shake. His thanks is plain and genuine for your role in saving the boat.

No, your crew didn't win a prize for the race, but what you carried away will shape the way you navigate challenges.

With that, the captain waves and makes his way along the dock. You stare at the crumpled paper and unfold it carefully. It reads:

**"What's worth more: the race you win,
or the course that changes you along the way?"**

At the bottom of the note is an anchor intertwined with a compass rose. The anchor's crossbar aligns with the east-west of the compass rose and the north point extends just above the anchor's ring. This image is the embodiment of direction and steadiness.

On the back side of the note, another message describes a fork in the journey, "There are more exciting and powerful lessons on the horizon. The choice is yours."

Choice One

Retreat to an ancient family farmstead in the Atlas Mountains, where silence becomes a teacher, and you'll discover what it means to feel truly well in your skin.

FIND CHAPTER 7: WELL IN YOUR SKIN • PAGE 69

Choice Two

Venture into the vibrant commotion of India, where amidst chai stalls and temple bells, you'll come face-to-face with wise counsel.

FIND CHAPTER 8: GOOD THING, BAD THING • PAGE 77
~~~~

Finding your treasured notebook in your backpack, you place the crumpled note between two pages. Looking up, you watch Captain Claus in his red overalls, duffle bag over his shoulder, disappear into the early dawn fog.

Now, it's time to venture toward another course that will change you along the way.

The Inner Harbor

DISCOVERING WHO YOU ARE

CHAPTER 6

The Value of Your Voice

How do you balance staying true to your values and passions while adapting to the demands of a new career and a professional environment?
AUNER M.

JULY, SEAFIELD & FILLYSIDE ROADS
EDINBURGH, SCOTLAND
55.9°N, 3.1°W

With short notice, a long-time friend from school invites you to join her on an adventure in Scotland. She's a couple of years older than you and you've always looked up to her. She swears the trip will be fun and budget friendly, and you are thrilled to receive the invite. Thankfully you have a few vacation days available, plus you think it would be good to get away from the grind. You accept the offer.

Though neither of you has ever driven on the left side of the road, you feel brave enough to try it, and your friend says she will navigate. In a rented subcompact car, you speed along narrow roads on the edge of the North Sea.

Supposedly, you are heading north toward St. Andrews, primarily known as the birthplace of the legendary sport of golf, an acronym "Gentlemen Only Ladies Forbidden" as you come to find out!

There is a light drizzle, typical for Scotland, and you search around the unfamiliar dashboard to cue the windshield wipers.

Out of nowhere, your friend announces she wants to take a more scenic route and stops the GPS. This makes you uncomfortable because your friend has never been on this route before. Though you aren't the navigator, you take note that heading north would mean the North Sea should be on your RIGHT, not your left.

You say the words out loud, quietly but with certainty, "The water should not be on our left."

With an assured voice, your friend directs you to go left, and then right, and then swirl around several roundabouts. The pit in your stomach grows larger with every turn of the steering wheel. You know you are heading the wrong way, and this is when you utter for a second time,

"The water should NOT be on our left."

There is a flurry of disagreement, horns honking, lights flashing, and a police siren that is meant for you.

You have run a red light.

Then, WHAM, crash, crunch!

Your car lurches forward, the inertia of your body is stopped by the seatbelt as it presses against your chest. With an opposing jolt you fling against the seatback.

Your car has been hit by a towering, grey, mechanic's truck. You're ok, but unsettled.

Your car is now an obstacle in the middle of the multi-lane intersection. Avoiding your friend's eyes, you lean your head back, and let out a long groan.

. . .

When there is a pit in your stomach, do you stop to figure out what is wrong? Do you make a point of expressing yourself when your intuition is telling you to speak up?

There are many reasons individuals remain silent: fear of dissent, avoidance of conflict, or a desire to appear aligned with the wishes of a perceived leader. Individuals may be pulled to make detrimental, dangerous, or even illegal decisions when there is a lack of trust to speak up.

There are hundreds of stories and high-profile cases that have ended tragically because individuals fell silent when they should have spoken up to redirect the situation.

Finding and using your voice effectively is a journey. It's tricky because you risk not being heard, disrespected, punished, ostracized, or making your current or future situation even more uncomfortable. By using your voice respectfully, you are acting as an advocate for yourself or someone else; neither especially easy, but necessary.

There are many examples from my own life when I either struggled to use my voice, did it poorly, and in some cases learned from my mistakes.

French Class

In college, my French professor gave me a failing grade of D, despite the fact that I always showed up early, led study groups, and joined every activity. No one worked harder. In the final week, he decided my entire grade would hinge on one essay he didn't like. I was furious, but I stayed silent. I never questioned him or spoke up for myself. The D is still on my transcript.

First Corporate Job

At my first corporate job, my manager promised to double my pay if

I met a list of goals. I hit every one quickly. But when I asked him about it later, he'd forgotten the deal. That's when I realized no one would advocate for my career but me. I scheduled a meeting, came prepared with proof, and spoke respectfully. It didn't fix everything, but it made one thing clear: I was serious about my growth and my career.

Fortune 500

In my first management role at a Fortune 500 company, my boss was a tyrant, publicly belittling me almost daily. I stayed silent, afraid to make things worse or show it bothered me. Looking back, I should have confronted him, or walked away from the situation.

Finding My Voice

Later, when a senior vice president role opened, I knew I was ready. Instead of applying online and waiting, I walked straight into the executive vice president's office, told him I wanted the job, and explained why I could deliver. My hands were shaking the whole time, but I was so glad I found the courage to speak up for myself. I got the job.

Frustration

During my time as a senior vice president, I hit a period of intense stress and fatigue. One afternoon, an employee came to my office with a client concern, and instead of being her advocate, I snapped. She fled in tears, and I recognized I'd let pressure override my empathy. I apologized immediately and meant it. From that moment on, I made a promise to myself to pause, breathe, listen with heart, and let clarity and respect steer my voice.

Feelings

Sharing feelings never came easily to me. For years, I couldn't tell close friends I loved them. When a mentor finally said she loved me, I replied, "Ditto." She was stunned because it felt like a trite response to her. It's ironic that I later needed open-heart surgery; maybe life was giving me a metaphor. Since then, I've learned to say what matters. Don't wait, use your voice to tell people they matter; they will benefit and so will you.

It's easy to think silence keeps peace; if we stay quiet, the moment will pass, and no one gets hurt. Silence, though, has a cost. Silence asks YOU to carry the weight of a truth that was meant to be shared.

When I look back, I realize my reticence to speak up was my attempt at protecting myself and others. On the one hand, this steers us away from conflict, rejection, and loss. When fear overprotects, on the other hand, it becomes a prison. Fears are valid, but courage isn't the absence of fear; it is recognizing which fear deserves to lead. Fear of conflict might protect your comfort; fear of losing your voice protects your SELF.

The longer we stay silent, the more we trade short-term comfort for long-term discomfort—the quiet kind that turns into resentment, self-doubt, or regret.

Speaking up isn't synonymous with attacking or winning; it's simply aligning your outer voice with your inner truth. Even if the outcome is messy, you've honored your personal integrity.

Silence has a cost and so does speaking carelessly. The goal isn't simply to speak up, but to speak well—with clarity, courage, and respect.

Finding your voice isn't about speaking louder; it's about speaking with purpose. Volume doesn't always equal substance. Know when to hold back, when to listen, and when to stand firm. Each choice builds confidence and defines who you become.

Claiming your voice doesn't happen in a vacuum. For some, speaking up is simply a matter of courage or practice; for others, it's complicated by lived experiences tied to gender, race, background, culture, family, or physical presence. Unfortunately, there is a long history around the world of power dynamics and privilege that shapes who is heard and who must work harder to be taken seriously.

While this story shines a light on strengthening your voice, we must acknowledge that not everyone begins on equal footing, and that some journeys may include unlearning messages that have taught them to remain silent. And for some, the real work in this chapter isn't about dominating with your voice, but learning to pause, listen deeply, and make space for others. That's a lesson of its own.

For now, this is an invitation to claim your voice in the way that feels true, safe, and grounded. Remember, that's a journey in itself that develops over time, even in small ways, and may just be the current that carries you to your next horizon.

. . .

Back in Scotland, police lights cast blue beams across the top of your car. Two officers in high-vis vests walk directly toward your door.

You've been in a traffic stop before and you've even had a fender bender before, but never at the same time. Also, you are concerned about which will take precedence in the eye of the law.

Getting stopped by the police, no matter where you are in the world, can stir a mix of emotions, nervousness, confusion, even fear—a true test of composure and character. It stirs something universal in us: the instinct to defend and yet the need to stay calm.

The moment asks for both presence and restraint: to stay respectful without surrendering your voice, to follow instructions while remembering you still have rights. How you handle those few minutes can either escalate tensions or build mutual understanding. The key is composure, breathing, listening carefully, and letting clarity, not adrenaline, guide your response.

You take a few seconds to breathe deeply and gain composure.

An officer taps on your window. You roll it down, and with every inch the glass descends you feel the blood draining from your face.

Breathlessly, you say sincerely, "I am so sorry, Officer. We are incredibly lost, and I am new to driving in Scotland."

They can tell by your accent that this statement is likely true. The officers eye you and then look toward your friend who is staring straight ahead.

At this point, the mechanic with a ponytail and baggy jeans emerges from the truck now linked to your bumper, yelling about the fact that the vehicle is owned by his boss and he may lose his job.

You continue in a respectful, measured tone, trying to maintain your composure, "It was my mistake, Officer. I misjudged the light. I should've stopped. He couldn't have avoided it. We're fine, just shaken."

One of the officers considers your sincerity and replies, "You've had a bit of a fright. Good that no one's hurt."

They ask you to get out of the car and exchange insurance information. In the sprinkling rain, you and your friend walk to the rear of the car, assess the damage, and snap a picture of it. You are relieved it is only a minor dent, but still you wish you had a magic dent eraser.

The mechanic with the ponytail approaches both of you.

Searching for shreds of courage, you say with respect and sincerity, "I've already told the police the truth, and I want you to hear it from me, too. You don't deserve to take the blame for something I caused. I'm truly sorry."

The anger in the mechanic's eyes softens, and he replies with appreciation for your words. Looking at your bumper, he says, "I have a dent repair kit in my truck. It would only take a minute to fix your bumper."

You are stunned at the turn of events. As the mechanic walks to the back of his truck, he says, "No mechanic carries every tool, just the ones that fit the job. Being prepared doesn't mean dragging extra weight; it means knowing what to pull from your toolbox when something breaks."

With that, Mr. Ponytail reveals the dent repair kit, and in a flash your rental car looks like new.

Relieved, you say, "How can I thank you?"

The mechanic replies, "You said you were sorry and meant it. That's enough for me."

The policeman closest to you, reaches in his clipboard tablet and hands you a folded yellow piece of paper. As they return to their squad car, one calls over his shoulder, "You should be careful and review the rules of the road. Remember, we drive on the left."

You can feel the onion skin yellow paper in your hands. Slowly unfolding, you read the rain-streaked note. It says,

**"You found your voice today—
with your friend, the officers, and the mechanic.
You spoke with honesty and respect,
and it calmed what panic could have stirred.
Then came the surprise:
the very person you stood up for
turned back to help you."**

You are stunned to see an embossed compass rose in the corner of the note.

A knowing smile spreads across your face, as you refold the paper. You find your treasured notebook, thrown to the floor of the car from the impact of the accident. Tracing the words *Aude Volāre,* you place the new note between two pages of the book.

PROPELLER PLAN Use Your Voice

Silence can feel safe, but it rarely steers you anywhere new. Remaining silent can chip away at your confidence, your relationships, and even your opportunities.

Speaking up doesn't mean shouting over others. It means learning to pause, listening to your inner compass, recognizing when you're wrong, and choosing words that carry truth and warrant respect. Even small course corrections in conversation can steer you toward healthier, more authentic connections.

Take a moment to reflect deeply:

1. **Personal Life.** Are there moments with family or friends where you swallow your words out of fear of conflict? Where would honesty bring healing, even if it feels uncomfortable at first?

2. **Professional Life.** Are you holding back ideas in meetings, thinking they're not good enough? Could your suggestion spark innovation, or prevent a mistake from being repeated?

3. **Your Story.** Have you ever let someone else narrate your direction because you didn't speak up about your values, boundaries, or dreams? What might change if you gave yourself permission to say them aloud?

4. **Looking Forward.** What new horizon might come into view if you dared to voice an idea that's been bubbling just below the surface?

Guidelines for Using Your Voice

1. **Lead with Calmness, Not Volume.** The goal of your voice is connection, not domination. Speak with clarity.

2. **Honor Humanity.** Respect opens more doors than aggression. Understanding is more important than being right. Listening shows you care.

CHOOSE-YOUR-CURRENT

One of the policemen returns and taps lightly on your window. With a look of respect, he says, "The 'Value Your Voice' lesson has found you, and with it, a turning point. Your journey deepens from here. Two choices await your selection."

Choice One

Journey to the edge of the African continent, where two mighty oceans collide and the waves slam the rocks below. You'll learn that depth comes from presence, not pace.

FIND CHAPTER 9: PLOT DEPTH AND DISTANCE • PAGE 87

Choice Two

Cover the vast expanse of the Grand Canyon, where rim-to-rim sunlit cliffs stretch endlessly and you learn that sometimes the only way forward is to set down what no longer serves you.

FIND CHAPTER 10: UNLOAD DEADWEIGHT • PAGE 97

The officer straightens his cap, gives a wry smile, then advises as he steps away, "**Make your choice, or the current will choose it for you.**" You watch him vanish into the fog and hit the road of potential.

CHAPTER 7

Well in Your Skin

I want to know how to be more loving and accepting of myself . . .
I struggle with absolutely tearing myself down when I make a mistake
and making myself feel dumb or like a loser or failure.
ANONYMOUS

MAY, ATLAS MOUNTAINS
LARBAÂ NATH IRATHEN, ALGERIA, AFRICA
36.6°N, 4.2°E

The needle scratches the surface of the record, emitting the warm sound of Maria Callas expertly singing Puccini's opera, Tosca. Opera isn't typically on your "go to" playlist, but somehow this music gives you goose bumps, in a good way. The waves of the soprano chords reach the dining nook where you are perched feasting your eyes on the foothills of the Atlas Mountain range.

You find yourself suspended in time, in the lush countryside near Larbaâ Nath Irathen, nestled in Algeria's northern Tizi Ouzou Province, just twenty-five miles from the shimmering Mediterranean Sea. Stories of this place drift back to you, tales of your grandfather's childhood, set among these same hills. A century ago, in the early 1900s, this town was known as Fort National, celebrated then, as now, for its majestic mountain vistas and enduring spirit.

Your grandfather's sister, Zana, bought the family property, a whitewashed retreat from another time, and is now renovating it into her home. During their youth, Aunt Zana and your Grandfather Muse toggled between the shores of France and Algeria. You learn they were called *pieds-noirs*, literally "black feet," referring to Europeans who lived in Algeria before 1962.

Aunt Zana asks if you would like to come help with the restoration if she pays for your flight. Without thinking twice, you launch toward the opportunity. Now, after a long but rewarding day of work, Aunt Zana sits across from you twirling her bangle bracelets, imitating the sounds of a windchime playing a blessing in the breeze. She gazes at some far away dream.

Placed on colorful plates before you, is an array of homemade sweets, topped off with a pot of rich, dark coffee. With your mouth full of pastry, you break the silence and mumble to your aunt, "You live in the most beautiful place in the world."

She casts you a knowing gaze and replies, "Si tu es bien dans ta peau."

Only if you *are well in your own skin.*

Aunt Zana wipes her round glasses, expounding on this famous philosophy.

She looks at you keenly and continues, "You must be well in your own skin to truly absorb the beauty of any moment."

The art of *well in your skin* is like a beautifully balanced three-legged stool where each leg is a state of wellbeing: physical, mental, and emotional. Wellness in your skin means being accepting, caring, authentic, and at ease.

A rush of chi energy sweeps through you, and you feel like you have been given the keys to the meaning of life.

Your aunt leaves her cup of coffee for a brief minute to flip the vinyl record. Once the second half of the opera starts playing, she returns to the table to select another tart. Between bites and falling crumbs, she continues her explanation of what it means to be *bien dans ta peau.*

To be well in your skin, ah, it is not about chasing youth. It's about speaking honestly of your journey . . . all of it . . . the good and the bad.

Beauty is not in your disguise but in your acceptance.

You must find your manner, your look, your rhythm that feels true, that feels . . . comfortable.

She pauses, giving a small shrug, the kind only someone like her could make seem philosophical.

Aunt Zana continues, "This advice is for everyone. To be at ease in your skin is a lifelong art, fluid and continuous, like a river that does not dry up with the years. You must learn to live at peace with yourself, whatever stage, whatever age."

You gaze back at the mountains with a new found perspective and begin to open your mind to being well in your skin.

· · ·

In our modern society, no matter how many articles and books are written about loving your body, body shaming still seems pervasive. "Being well in your skin" is easier said than done. We live in a world where filters can erase pores, algorithms can amplify insecurity, and entire industries profit off of marketing messages that the natural body is not enough.

Let's be honest, the pressure is real, and nobody wakes up every day loving every angle of themselves.

What helped me begin accepting my own body shape wasn't a magic moment; it was building a daily habit of gratitude. Gratitude for a body that does its job of walking, breathing, creating, and letting me be there for the people who matter.

I have a friend who lost one of his legs in his thirties while serving in the military. Amazingly, he always has a big smile on his face and talks openly about his gratitude for his remaining leg and for the prosthesis that allows him to run marathons.

When you shift from critiquing your body to appreciating what it lets you do, the noise of perfectionism loses some of its grip.

Surround yourself with people who don't treat appearance like a scoreboard. Seek out communities of friends, mentors, and creators, who normalize real bodies, real emotions, and real life. They will appreciate that same grace from you.

Curate your social feed like your mental health depends on it (because it does). Mute or unfollow accounts that trigger comparison spirals, and choose content that affirms, educates, and brings you joy.

And perhaps most importantly, aim for a lifestyle that supports the long game: sleep that restores, movement that energizes, food that nourishes, and a pace that doesn't burn you out. Wellness isn't chasing an aesthetic; it is learning to fuel your body with kindness and honesty.

It wasn't until I was in the middle of my career that I started to embrace my shape and size and worked toward understanding the art and science of being well in my skin. Pointing at the deep crease between my eyebrows, I would announce, "I will not cover up these wrinkles. I have worked too hard for these."

It wasn't a joke.

In my forties, just as I was hitting my stride, life surprised me with a near-death experience. An unknown virus attacked my heart, and I collapsed just after a client meeting in Maine. My young, athletic, and energetic body was in a blur of shock laying flat on a gurney as I was pulled into heart surgery resulting in an 8-inch red scar, every inch a titanium wire protruding under the skin to bind my sternum.

After that near death experience, I had to reevaluate. Could I still be well in my own skin, scar and all? After surgery, I asked a dermatologist and friend what kind of cream I should put on the scar to help it heal. Her response was profound, one I will never forget.

She said, "It doesn't matter what cream you put on your scar. It is the act of caring touch that will help it heal."

Her words stunned me and I grappled with the incredible power of that statement, especially coming from a doctor.

The act of caring touch is healing!

When human touch comes from a place of genuine care, asking for nothing in return, it becomes something sacred. It's the quiet language of presence, offered with sincerity and received with trust. It doesn't seek to claim or to fix. It simply says, "I'm here with you." Its power lies not in complexity, but in the simplicity of connection.

If caring touch heals scars, what else can caring touch do? From this advice, I have continued the learning process of being well in my own skin no matter the time, no matter the place, no matter the age, no matter the scars, no matter the circumstances.

It is in this state of wellness that you can be present . . . really present. In the moment, take in great beauty, look for marks of wonder, connect deeply with those around you, and be open to the mystery of what unfolds.

• • •

Within the stone walls of the 19th century *djenan* (garden farmhouse in paradise), the record stops, and the silence allows this *well in your own skin* message to penetrate beneath the surface.

Aunt Zana leans forward with one hand supporting her chin. She continues to punctuate the message, "Becoming well in your own skin is less about fixing yourself and more about befriending yourself. It's learning to ignore the noise and choosing to live authentically, building a life you love that is true, steady, and aligned from the inside out."

Aunt Zana looks at you to see if the message is resonating. With a twinkle in her eye she says, "Tend to your body and spirit like you would a close friend. Rest when you're tired. Eat what nourishes you. Move in ways that feel alive. Laughter, creativity, and solitude all count as self-care. Wellness grows in the small, consistent ways you honor your own needs."

Soaking in her wise counsel, you once again look toward the rolling foothills of the Atlas Mountains. This time, they appear even more beautiful than when you first mentioned this home in paradise.

You take your last sip of coffee. The day is passing faster than expected, and your cousin arrives to take you to dinner. Aunt Zana stands to greet your cousin and kisses your cheeks in a farewell embrace. She sneaks a folded piece of paper into your palm.

Smiling slyly and with a wink, she says, "See you tomorrow. Come ready to work."

Once in your cousin's car, you carefully unfold the delicate paper. It is scrawled with a style of handwriting from a time passed. It reads,

"Caring touch has its own quiet healing power. Be yourself. Keep your sense of humor. And above all, do what helps you feel at home in your own skin—no judgment, no self-punishment, just grace."

You smile at the last bit and mindfully relax your body. You know the trifecta of wellness (physical, emotional, mental) won't be easy, but you can see it will be worth the effort, especially if it means truly absorbing the beauty of any moment.

Refolding the paper, you notice a coffee ring smudge at the bottom of the note. Perhaps Grandfather Muse has always been with you in spirit. Thinking about this notion, you find your treasured notebook in your backpack, and press the note between two pages. You will think about this later. For now, you are ready for couscous and an enjoyable evening with your cousin.

PROPELLER PLAN The Feeling Well in Your Skin Journey

To be well in your own skin is to carry both lightness and depth. It is not about erasing the years or fitting yourself into someone else's mold, but about honoring the story your body and spirit already tell. True beauty comes when you embrace your natural self, lines that speak of laughter and scars that whisper resilience.

Take time to pause and consider these points:

1. Embrace Every Version of You. What parts of myself have I learned to accept, and what parts am I still resisting?

2. Speak Gratitude Over Critique. Do I treat my body and spirit with gratitude, or am I self-critical? What small course correction could help me find gratitude for the things I have?

3. Identify with Presence Over Performance. Where do I feel pressure to perform or pretend? What does the authentic me look like and how can I find ways to share that?

4. Tend to Your Wellbeing. Do I take enough time to practice gentle self-care: a walk, a delicious meal, or laughter with a friend?

5. Walk in True Confidence. How might my presence change if I moved through the world with genuine confidence and respect rather than constant comparison?

Remember: being at ease in your own skin is not a fixed destination but a continuous voyage. The tide rises and falls, and so too does your confidence. Each moment offers another chance to return to self-acceptance.

<div align="center">~~~~~</div>

CHOOSE-YOUR-CURRENT

While still in the driveway of your aunt's ancient home, she raps on the car window just as you and your cousin are about to leave. She exclaims, "An adventure awaits if you are open to it."

Choice One

Fly to South Africa and visit the tip of the continent where you will learn to walk with the path rather than forcing speed and conquest.

FIND CHAPTER 9: PLOT DEPTH AND DISTANCE • PAGE 87

Choice Two

Settle into your new life in Kansas City: new job, new townhouse, new city. Between a questionable real estate investment and work demands, you discover what it means to recharge your battery and find strength that lasts.

FIND CHAPTER 11: RECHARGE YOUR BATTERY • PAGE 107

Her words hanging heavy in the air, your aunt waves goodbye and ambles back to her sanctuary.

CHAPTER 8

Good Thing, Bad Thing

*I want to know how to overcome being overwhelmed, the stress it brings
when you feel you aren't "good enough" or where "you should be."
How do I not compare my success to others and dwell on how
fast others transition into their career successfully?*
ROSHAY F.

**APRIL, LOTUS TEMPLE
DELHI, INDIA
28.7°N, 77.1°E**

In dusty sandals, you stroll through Delhi's Khari Baoli market feeling as if you've landed head-first into a bottomless spice sack. Your senses are captivated by street vendors frying samosas, rickshaws weaving aimlessly through traffic, and stray dogs sneaking a forgotten piece of meat. The rich scents ascend your mind to a realm only experienced by mystics.

The hum of activity is much easier to navigate if you envision yourself swimming alongside a school of playful fish in an undulating sea. You remember hearing the street activity described as swirls versus grids and believe that is an accurate description.

At the end of the market, a towering temple stands proud, supported by its ancient roots. Columns of red, blue, and gold mimic the colors of the sacks of spices. It's almost as if the vendors painted the giant beauty in the hues of their harvest.

Your thoughts are interrupted by the suggestion, "Please remove your shoes."

Startled, you look up and see a portly man dressed in a white tunic. A broad smile has taken permanent residence on his face. You stare for too long and he repeats himself, "Please remove your shoes out of reverence and place them here."

He gestures at bins lined in perfect order, rising halfway to the ceiling. Snapping to attention, you join a queue of wordless worshippers who apparently know the rules of the occasion and are filing toward the welcoming entrance, and you follow suit by removing your shoes.

Before you arrive at the grand double doors, there is a fountain of pure water flowing like a river over white marble. In an act of reverence, each man and woman steps through the fountain to wash their feet before they enter the temple. You've never seen this observance or formality before, but are quite taken by the symbolic gesture.

The cool and dim interior is in stark contrast to the boiling May day. You've been longing for a monsoon rainfall, but hear that it won't come for another month. Inside the cavernous room there is a small stage where a group is playing instruments you've never seen before, but the lilting music is already soothing and cleansing your body much like the flowing stream. You find your way to an ornate rug stitched in the same colors as the exterior walls and, mimicking the other devotees, sit cross legged on the floor.

The music stops. One of the musicians stands and walks toward the edge of the stage. You are enthralled by how easily he rises and moves, as if the foundations of youth have taken everlasting residence in his bones and skin. In silence, he looks thoughtfully at each devotee.

Drawing breath, he says softly, *"Good thing? Bad thing? Who knows?"*

He continues, "Things are only *good* or *bad* because we define them as so.

"Sometimes we are tempted to describe what seems to be a terrible event as a very *bad thing*: a traffic jam, a missed flight, an unsatisfactory review, a letter of rejection, or an empty bank account. At the moment, each of these individual events seems like a very *bad thing*, and our physical body mimics our thoughts: a burning stomach, a raging headache, or a stye in our eye.

"Is it really a *bad thing*? Sometimes, given time and space and the unfolding of new events, a painful past event may, and can, develop into a very good thing."

With that you grab your notebook out of your backpack and try to scribble the essence of these meaningful words. As if dictating, you continue to scribe to the page the wisdom coming from the guru's mouth.

His words continue, "There is a powerful example of this truth in a folk parable with ancient roots."

The wise speaker lowers himself to the edge of the stage and sits with his hands on his knees. He begins the story, "A young sailor and an old captain set out to sea with a steady breeze at their back.

"By nightfall, the wind died down, leaving them stranded on a still, glassy ocean.

"'What a bad thing,' the sailor muttered.

"'Who knows,' said the old captain beside him.

"As they drifted, the sailor repaired his frayed sails and mended his lines. Days later, when the wind returned, their ship flew faster than ever reaching a distant island rich with goods for trade.

"'What a good thing,' the sailor exclaimed!

"'Who knows,' said the old captain.

"On their return, a sudden gale threw their newly acquired cargo overboard.

"'What a bad thing,' the sailor screamed.

"'Who knows,' said the old captain.

"Yet the lightened ship skimmed safely into harbor.

"'What a good thing,' said the relieved sailor.

"'Who knows,' said the old captain."

The guru smiles at his spellbound audience and continues, "Fortune drifts like the tide; loss may simply be the current bringing you back to what is meant for you."

. . .

Just before COVID, I was knocked off course by a sudden squall, peaking in a figurative shipwreck. The pain in my chest was like a giant hydraulic spreader widening and widening, threatening to tear my ribs away from my sternum and spine. Gripping my chest in pain, I collapsed at the emergency room door of the hospital.

My athletic body was battling a viral attack which poured a liter of fluid around my heart, threatening to stop it from beating. With alarm bells, code red announcements, beeping monitors, and emergency surgery, I found myself in cardiac critical care. This moment seemed like a "very bad thing."

Little did I know this pit would become the catalyst for some of the most amazing experiences I would have NEVER had otherwise. What seemed like the worst moment of my life became the interruption that opened the doors for possibility. The viral attack on my heart forced a hard stop and reset on my life.

Good thing? Bad thing? Who knows?

In that stillness, lying in bed for months on end, the noise of ambition and routine fell away, and I was left with stark clarity: if my days are limited, how do I truly want to spend them? That brush with mortality rewrote my priorities and stripped away any illusion that there would always be more time.

Out of that stillness came permission and courage.

Permission to pivot away from the safe and expected, and the courage to claim titles I once thought impossible—artist, professor, writer, speaker, van lifer. Each found identity was born from the realization that the greater risk was not trying!

Although, it's not necessary to wait for a crisis to awaken your truth, without it I likely would have stayed on my frenetic, narrow path. With it, the "bad thing" became a very "good thing" and the horizon revealed beautiful opportunities I would have never otherwise seen. What had originally seemed like an ending became a beginning more expansive than I could have ever imagined.

Would I want to go through open heart surgery again? No, absolutely not. I am, however, 100 percent grateful it happened and wouldn't change it for the world. My near-death experience turned into a very good thing.

Now, whenever I am faced with an event, from traffic snarls to illnesses that I am tempted to call a bad thing, I reframe my focus and say, "Good thing, bad thing? Who knows!"

Remember, it is only a bad thing when we label it so.

This kind of thinking suspends judgment and can be an amazing stress reliever!

There is one more interesting parallel to my emergency heart surgery day. My friend and my sister came to my aid when I called in desperation. My friend had a plane to catch for a business meeting, and when she knew I was safely in the arms of the doctors, she ran to the airport, dreadfully late and in danger of missing her flight. She swam through the sea of passengers at the TSA security check and begged to edge toward the front of the line.

One angry passenger yelled at her, "You should get up earlier, lady!"

Little did he know that she was only late because she had spent hours helping to save my life.

It is a graceful way to live when we suspend judgment.
We have no idea what is going on in someone else's life.
When we say, "Good thing, bad thing? Who knows?" we suspend judgment for ourselves . . . and grow further by suspending judgment for others too.

. . .

The guru in the temple continues, "The ancient Sufis often mused, 'If you are distressed by anything external, the pain is not due to the thing itself, but to your estimate of it; and this, you have the power to revoke at any moment.'

"Pain is inevitable. Suffering is optional."

The guru stands and begins walking around the room, "Because life often reveals meaning in hindsight, what feels like loss or failure in the moment can be the very thing that strips away what's holding us back, redirecting us to new opportunities, and revealing strengths we never knew we had. The very thing that seemed the worst becomes the doorway to what's best."

You pause and think to yourself, "That's right!" You write in your notebook, "What seems the worst in the moment may become the best thing for our future."

After the service in the sacred temple, you find the guru to express gratitude for the powerful impact of his words. You stand quietly in the presence of his wisdom, turning the mantra over like a smooth stone in your hand.

At last, you state, "I wonder how my life might look differently if I could truly live this lesson?"

The guru smiles, eyes crinkling with kindness.

> **"Your life will never be without storms, but you will sail**
> **with trust, knowing each new wind carries you closer**
> **to who you are meant to become."**

Then handing you a note, he bows, and bids you, "Namaste, the sacred in me recognizes the sacred in you." He turns to leave the temple and fades into the crowds on the narrow street of the swirling spice market.

PROPELLER PLAN Wisdom in Saying "Who Knows"

Life rarely warns you whether an event will be a blessing or a burden. What looks like a setback today may carry the seed that blooms tomorrow's opportunity. When we rush to label our circumstances as good or bad, we get caught in our preconceived judgments, ignoring possibilities. Sometimes it takes distance, days, years, or even decades to see how a storm will redirect us to richer shores.

Pause and consider:

1. **Rethink Bad.** Where am I too quick to label something as "bad?" Is it possible it might be the start of something "good?"

2. **Find Gifts in Disappointment.** What past disappointment turned out to be an unexpected opportunity?

3. **Pay It Forward.** Who could benefit from my support as they navigate life's curve balls?

Wisdom often lives in the space of "Who knows?" Holding that posture of curiosity allows room for grace to work unseen.

CHOOSE·YOUR·CURRENT

You open the thin colorful paper held together with a wax seal. The words are written in ink and calligraphy. It says,

"Judge less, trust more. Every current, whether gentle or fierce, moves you toward the horizon that is yours to discover. Two choices now lie ahead; let your spirit choose which tide to follow."

Choice One

Venture through the vast rim-to-rim wilds of the Grand Canyon, discovering that the surest way forward is to let go of the weight holding you back.

FIND CHAPTER 10: UNLOAD DEADWEIGHT • PAGE 97

Choice Two

Begin again in Kansas City, balancing an exciting new job with the deadlines of renovating your townhouse. A professional development event shows you how to "recharge your battery" and restore lasting strength.

FIND CHAPTER 11: RECHARGE YOUR BATTERY • PAGE 107

Considering your options, you study the blue wax seal imprinted with a compass rose. You gaze toward the ornate ceiling and believe that Grandfather Muse is looking down upon you. With your treasured notebook still in your hands, you trace the words,

"Aude Volāre"

You wonder at the meaning while safeguarding the note between two pages.

Deep in thought, you close the tome and follow the steps of the guru out into the unfolding street, where your new understanding helps you ride the current alongside the school of fish.

⚓

SECTION V

Preparing the Vessel

LIGHTER,
STRONGER,
STEADY

CHAPTER 9

Plot Depth and Distance

I often feel behind in life and behind my peers.
JENNIFER D.

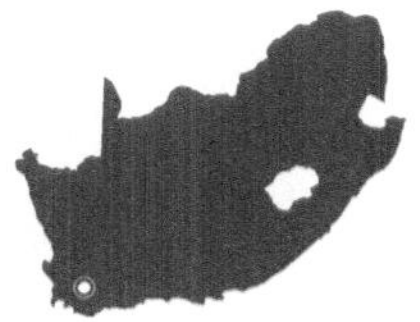

JUNE, MUIZENBERG BEACH
CAPE TOWN, SOUTH AFRICA
33.9°S, 18.4°E

Over dinner one night, your friend tells you she is traveling to Cape Town for work. You jump at the opportunity to join her, especially because there is a free hotel room and you can check off a new country on your list. In the days before the flight, you make a checklist of must-see attractions: ride the Hop-On-Hop-Off Bus (yes, it's touristy, but you love it), experience Khadim's traditional coffee ceremony, eat your way through Mojo Market, listen to the Ghetto Sessions musical extravaganza, plus a seat at the Table Mountain to watch the sunset.

The fifteen-hour flight is the longest you've ever endured, and you have a roster of eight in-flight movies under your belt to prove it! When the plane's wheels hit the ground, you are ready to sprint to the starting line of your adventures, but your brakes squeal when you realize your suitcase is missing from the carousel. A diatribe of anger is unleashed in your head, and you are glad no one can read your mind. This is not the way you hoped to begin your vacation.

After standing in an eternal queue to instigate a search for your long-lost contents, the agent looks at her papers and says with a lack of sympathy, "You should see your bag in a few days."

A few days! This news cramps your style, literally—you'll have nothing to wear! By the time you receive your suitcase you'll have seen everything in Cape Town. In a few days you could be as far as Kruger Park or maybe even Victoria Falls. You have people to see and places to go.

Taking a deep breath, you head for the safety of the airport bathroom. The mirror reflects hair in need of combing, and your brown sweat suit ready for the laundry. The soft material was perfect comfort for a long haul flight, but is certainly not the sexy number you were hoping for when meeting new people. You don't even have clean underwear or socks.

At the airport exit, your friend yanks your arm and says, "Who cares about your bag. You look fine. Let's meet my colleagues at the beach."

She pulls you to a waiting cab, and you notice with surprise the chilly June wind. You forgot the weather in the Southern Hemisphere is surfing toward winter, not summer. Too bad your jacket is in your lost bag!

At Muizenberg Beach, you note the brightly colored huts lining the southern coast. The red flag is waving, signaling a shark is lurking in the nearby waters and it isn't safe to swim. You cringe at the thought of ever wading in that surf, but it's only a short detour for your friend's colleagues who are waiting for the "all clear."

Since you have no interest in swimming, the red flag gives you the green light to leave the surfing area and visit the Cape of Good

Hope, once believed to be the southernmost tip of Africa. The others in your group have visited this landmark many times, so they offer to hold your spot on the beach, joking that they'll keep the sharks from eating your biltong and bunny chow lunch.

To you, going to the Cape of Good Hope sounds like the perfect opportunity for posting new content online, and bragging rights when you return home in real life. You learn that the Cape was first navigated in 1487 by a Portuguese ship attempting to establish direct trade relations with the Far East. That piques your interest, and you make a mental note to find out more. For now, you need to quickly get to the lookout point before closing time and back to your group, but with your eagerness you're sure you can do it.

You wave goodbye to your new friends, calling out, "I will be there now, now," the colloquial South African phrase implying a swift return.

In record time, you sprint from the beach through the Cape's visitor parking lot, past the oystercatcher birds and penguins, to the jagged cliffs where you believe the Indian and Atlantic Oceans converge. Taking your final step on the edge of the peninsula, you peer down the 650-foot cliff for a vapor-minute and quickly turn around to begin the return journey to your friends at the beach before they even know you're gone.

As you take your first step, a blind man with a cane and his guide cut in front of you and begin their own treacherous shuffle to the base. Your speed is halted by their unsteady steps, slowly . . . slowly. The path leading from the peak to the parking lot is steep and long, extremely narrow, and lined with rocks and sharp bushland thickets.

For minutes-on-end, you tow behind the pair, and frustratingly the narrow footpath holds your pace with a tight reign. Unable to pass the duo, you grow impatient with this crawling pace; it makes you feel like you are rowing in mud.

Finally, in the distance you see a fork in the trail, and you grow excited thinking the new route might also lead to the park's entrance. The ambling pair veer left, so you turn right hoping you can make up for lost time.

Your new trail winds up and down, passes more chirping penguins, a wall of rocks and more thicket, skirts to the right, and draws to a DEAD END at the grounds keeper's garage.

Your supposed shortcut is thwarted!

Through clenched teeth you exclaim out loud to no one in particular, "You've got to be kidding me!"

· · ·

For two decades as a national sales representative in financial services, I lived like a speedboat, quickly passing through ports. Whenever a meeting took me to a new city, I made it my mission to make an appearance at the local landmarks. Never enough time, I'd sprint from one site to another, snap the photo, check the figurative box, and rush back to catch my flight.

On the surface, it looked impressive, miles logged, cities visited, stories collected. But in truth, I was skimming across the water without ever lowering the anchor.

I was living for the moment instead of in the moment.

New York City, boat to the Statue of Liberty—check.

San Francisco, bike across the Golden Gate Bridge—check.

Boulder, experience the Frozen Dead Guy Days—check.

Fort Lauderdale, drive across Alligator Alley—check.

Fargo, view the woodchipper from the namesake movie—check.

With each extra moment, I quickly explored the horizons of all fifty U.S. states in record time—check, check and check.

According to Pew Research in 2016, about half of Americans said they're usually trying to do two or more things at once and 60% of U.S. adults said they at least sometimes feel too busy to enjoy life.[14] *Like most Americans, I was addicted to the adrenaline of a fast-paced lifestyle, running on high, and surfing from one compulsive wave to the next.*

It has taken years to unlearn that pace, to realize that depth is found when you pause long enough to explore below the surface, when you dive in rather than just sail above.

Depth reveals what endurance alone cannot, the quiet pulse and new meaning discovered beneath the motion. It's where discovery peers inward, shaping who you become.

Now, I try to live with a "both/and" mindset: to BOTH cover distance AND seek depth, to chase new horizons while also being fully present when I arrive. Because when your voyage is measured only in miles, you risk missing the treasures hidden in the depths.

• • •

Foiled by the dead end, nature forces you to retrace your steps. You find your way back to the fork, and this time take the well-traveled option. To your surprise, you once again find yourself exasperated behind the blind man with his cane and guide; slowly, slowly ambling down the path, as if time doesn't exist.

In a grand paradox, the unhurried pair arrive at the park entrance before you do.

The guide to the blind man turns toward you with the brightest smile, disarming your impatience. He says to you in a lilting South African accent, "Isn't the trek to the Cape life changing?"

Almost as a reminder to himself, he continues to his companion, "I find that if I quiet the outside noise and narrow my focus, bringing it to the present, then I can preserve my energy for what truly matters."

Interrupting, you ask sincerely, "What truly matters?"

The guide gives you a knowing look and then responds thoughtfully, "That is for you to decide and one of the great mysteries of life."

"For me, it's people," he continues. "Family, friends, new friends, yet to be friends; even people who are difficult. Because it is these relationships that give life rich meaning, depth, and growth."

You sense the strong bond he shares with his companion.

In an instant, the fog lifts from the chaos you had mistaken for purpose. You now see how relentlessly you have been chasing "progress:" career, money, new experiences, as if somehow this never-ending pursuit gives your life more meaning.

The guide then hands you a piece of paper. On the front it says,

"Life is about depth, not just distance."

The words *depth, not just distance* drive home a new concept for you. Your thoughts collide. The blind man and his guide win the prize for both depth AND distance, arriving at the entrance before you.

The guide turns to assist his companion, and they amble away.

Curious, you thoughtfully unfold the note and it says,

"Faster isn't always better. More isn't always more.
Deliberately cultivate depth, not just distance,
in both moments and relationships."

The guide turns to wave at you from a distance. You return the wave and smile. After watching the pair continue their stroll arm-in-arm, you refold the sea-sprayed note.

You've got it, *Cultivate depth, not just distance, in both moments and relationships.*

Deep in thought, you purposefully slow down as you make your way back to your friends on the beach. You ask yourself, "How would today have been different if I had intentionally cultivated depth?"

You could have deepened the relationships with your new friends.

You could have lingered to take a few deep breaths, inhaling the energy radiating from the two oceans converging.

You could have gained deeper insights from the blind man and his guide.

You catch yourself mid-thought, realizing that in your rush to conquer miles, you've only skimmed the surface of an experience that begged to be savored. You consider retracing the path to the Cape of Good Hope, to do it "right" this time. But, as the notion takes shape, a gentler truth settles in: perhaps depth isn't found by going back, but by being present in the here and now.

Back at the beach, you look at the arc of new friends seated beside you, the circle warm with laughter. Breathing in the salt scented air, you vow to stay present. One by one, you recapture the names of your new friends, letting the syllables roll on your tongue with reverence to etch them in your memory: Tlhogi, Thula, Xoliswa, Kgosi.

As if for the first time, you feel the wind in your hair and see the surf shimmer a deep, inky green; the food is alive with spice and depth. You sense the quiet miracle of connection. At this moment, you're not thinking about your lost luggage or your next stop. You're here, present inside this chapter of your story.

The journey you were chasing has already begun.

You dig in your backpack for your treasured notebook to safekeep the inspiring note from the Cape trail guide and his companion.

PROPELLER PLAN Cultivating Depth

It's easy to treat life like a checklist. In our frenetic world, we are tempted to rush from one thing to the next, skimming the surface of moments without ever sinking into them. Depth requires something more rare: presence. It asks us to notice, to linger, to put away the phone and look up, to give our full attention to the people and places right in front of us.

Before you proceed, note the following:

1. Focus on Presence Over Proximity. When was the last time you were with someone but weren't truly with them? What pulled your attention away?

2. Find Power in a Pause. How might that moment have felt different if you had slowed down and been fully present?

3. Give the Gift of Attention. Who in your life would flourish if you gave them your undivided attention, even just for a few minutes?

4. Notice Wonder. What beauty or wonder might you be missing among your surroundings because you're focused on the next best thing?

5. Seize Opportunities Within Reach. What career or professional development opportunities might you be overlooking?

6. Measure Depth. If you measured the value of your days by depth of your experience, how would tomorrow look different?

Pause here. Imagine, starting now, instead of doing more, dive deeper. When we are present and embrace depth, our lives grow richer and more meaningful as a result.

CHOOSE-YOUR-CURRENT

Placing the guide's message into your notebook, you realize there is a second page. You unfurl it to read, "Lessons rise from the depths to shape your voyage. Two paths open before you, step in, if your spirit is ready."

Choice One

Take a trip into the swirl of San Francisco's Global Software Conference, where each encounter is a guiding star, and mentors emerge to help steer you through the seas of opportunity.

FIND CHAPTER 12: CREWMATES · PAGE 119

Choice Two

Dive into Roatán's turquoise waters in Honduras, where fear gives way to wonder when a steady hand shows you how trust makes courage possible.

FIND CHAPTER 13: FIGHT, FLIGHT, OR FLOAT · PAGE 127

You write in your notebook,

> **"No matter which direction I choose,**
> **I must remember to be present and use these**
> **lessons to cultivate depth in my own life."**

You smile, noticing a compass rose with a coffee smudge like a watermark on the note. It makes you think somehow your Grandfather Muse is guiding your path.

CHAPTER 10

Unload Deadweight

*I have been grappling with the idea that I need to cut off some of my old
friends who are not doing productive things with their lives.*

LIAM G.

**NOVEMBER, NORTH RIM
GRAND CANYON, ARIZONA U.S.A.
36.2°N, 112.1°W**

Your adventurous cousin, Cliff, invites you to hike the Grand
Canyon from rim to rim in Arizona. Though harrowing, this is an invitation you can't pass up, especially because you don't want your
younger cousin to show you up. This invitation means descending
8,800 feet down the North Rim, crossing the canyon for three days,
and then ascending 7,000 feet straight up the South Rim. You think,
*It is like using the stair master at the gym for five straight days, but
the surroundings will be more beautiful.*

Over millennia, the Colorado River cut an immense hole in the
earth running the length of 277 miles, giving the Grand Canyon its
name. Because of the intensity of the hike, less than 1 percent of the

park's visitors attempt the trek from the North Rim to the South Rim, and a special permit is required.

Excited and nervous, you make a list of everything you'll need for the five days: a tent, a stove and pans, enough food and snacks for each day, five liters of water per day, five changes of clothes plus rain gear, a head lamp, a mattress pad, a water filtration kit, toilet paper and an excrement shovel (yes, really), ice cleats, bear spray, a snake bite kit and a bottle of bourbon in case you need to cleanse a wound (or at least that's what you tell your mother).

Some of these items are just in case, but you'd rather be overly prepared.

To make a bit of extra money for your trip, you work all day and book the last flight out the evening before the hike. You arrive in Arizona blurry-eyed and scattered. Once at the entrance of the national park, you intend to leave your car and take the bus with your cousin to the North Rim trailhead.

Because of your very late night, you are running behind and arrive just five minutes before the scheduled bus departure. In a whirlwind you tear through your suitcase and quickly throw the myriad of jumbled items from your list into your trail backpack.

There is one problem.

You can't lift your pack!

Literally.

The backpack is bulging and unbearably heavy.

Your cousin, Cliff, eyes you knowingly but is kind enough not to say anything.

• • •

Sometimes it's not the miles ahead that slow you down, it's the baggage you insist on dragging with you. Before #VanLife became a hashtag-worthy lifestyle, I decided to drive a Sprinter van named Millicent across the U.S. and paint the horizon in all fifty states.

My packing list? More like a packing spreadsheet that ran nearly 200 rows long, because apparently, I thought I was prepping for both a cross-country road trip and an apocalypse. Plus, if Lewis and Clark had Excel, you know they would've done the same.

Needs versus wants? Please. Obviously, I "needed" a full wardrobe for every season, plus dress clothes, because you never know when a black-tie gala might pop up at a KOA campground. (Spoiler alert: it didn't.)

And footwear? Let's just say I could've opened a roadside shoe store. Sneakers, hiking shoes, tall boots, sandals, flip flops, and yes, cowboy boots. Because really, how could I drive out West without them? That would've been downright un-American, maybe even sacrilegious.

Next came the accoutrements, because apparently, I wasn't just road-tripping. I was outfitting for an expedition. A yoga mat was non-negotiable (because nothing says inner peace like downward dog position between eighteen-wheelers). Hiking poles? Absolutely. And, naturally, a kayak, since clearly the only thing safer than being alone in the wilderness is being alone in the wilderness on water.

Then came the creature comforts: a giant fan in case Millicent morphed into a rolling sauna, a mosquito net in case she doubled as a bug buffet, and enough sun shades to rival a NASA launch pad.

And for mornings? Coffee prep became a full-blown identity crisis: French press, pour-over, drip brew. Why settle on one method when you can cart around all three? I even packed enough mugs and plates to host a dinner party. (Shockingly, no one RSVP'd.) I may have even packed a partridge in a pear tree; but I can't remember.

For safety, I brought along a pellet gun and a TASER, obviously useful tools for warding off, say, an aggressive truck-stop yogi or an overly curious alligator during a solo kayak. Can you tell I'm being facetious? Thankfully, both weapons stayed unused in their hiding spots, which meant my most dangerous encounters were with mosquitoes and questionable gas station burritos.

But hey, at least I was prepared for a black-tie gala with alligators, hosted in the desert, catered with coffee, and topped off with a cowboy line dance.

By the time I'd finished packing, Millicent looked less like a road-trip van and more like a traveling yard sale. All that gear, and yet the most important cargo was still me, white-knuckled behind the wheel, wondering how on earth I was going to drive this beast into the adventure of a lifetime.

I lasted exactly ONE day on the road before realizing I couldn't move around the living space I'd created, let alone find anything. To open the bathroom door, I had to wrestle a giant fan out of the way. To lie down, I had to shuffle past the yoga mat, hiking poles, a ball gown, and stack of plates. Every time I turned a corner on the road, there was a thunderous avalanche of stuff crashing from one side of the van to the other, like Millicent was a maraca, shaking me aware of my bad decisions.

Something had to give.

When I reached Pennsylvania, I pulled up to the first FedEx and shipped home half of my so-called "essentials." Suddenly, the road, my van, and I felt a whole lot lighter, literally and figuratively. I could breathe! It was no longer necessary to get a running start to close drawers packed with non-essentials, nor make the painful decision which coffee style to make, nor tangle with a pile of overstuffed throw pillows each time I wanted to enjoy a slow meal.

Millicent, the former traveling yard sale, was now rebranded as a minimalist's sanctuary on wheels. If I hadn't lightened the load, the van might've stalled out somewhere in Nebraska under the weight of my "just in case" lifestyle.

Because the path was now clear inside and out, we rolled on for 45,000 miles, I painted the horizon in all fifty states . . . and not once did I need the ball gown!

· · ·

History is full of reminders that carrying too much can come at a cost. My overstuffed van was more comedy than catastrophe, but for many explorers, the weight they refused to surrender became their undoing. Time and again, expeditions and venturers alike—brave, prepared, even legendary—have stalled or failed under the weight of unnecessary burdens. The stories that follow illustrate how excess can derail even the most determined operation.

1812—Napoleon's Retreat from Moscow [15]

The French Army invaded Russia with nearly 600,000 men. The army's discipline started to wane, and over time, the soldiers looted gold and religious icons from churches and government buildings which they stashed load after load onto their wagon trains. The sheer weight slowed their movement and made them easy targets.

Additionally, their obsession with the loot became disastrous when their distraction led them to overlook necessary provisions for winter. The men were ill-prepared and ran out of food and protective gear. Only ten percent of the army survived.

1897—Klondike Gold Rush [16]

Tens of thousands of people went to seek fortune during the 1897 Gold Rush in western Canada, just a few hundred miles from present day Alaska. There were no roads or transportation to and from the area where gold was found, so individuals had to hike over the mountains through thick snow and ice with their supplies in tow.

Many of the stampeders, as they were called because of their sheer number, treated the journey as if they were moving house rather than facing the inhospitable Arctic wilderness. Their "superfluous" items often revealed inexperience, optimism, or plain denial about what lay ahead. Dramatically overestimating what they could carry, many brought silverware, china dishes, even pianos and organs, bathtubs, feather beds and mattresses, and, the pièce de résistance, tuxedos and ballgowns. Their stories are a haunting testament to the lethal combination of greed and inexperience resulting in thousands of deaths.

In tribute to those who perished, a saloon in Dawson City, Yukon, the heart of the Gold Rush, still serves a cocktail known as the "Sourtoe." The recipe? A shot of whiskey, garnished with a real, mummified human toe. No joke. It's the town's most chilling toast to history.

1912—South Pole Expedition [17]

In 1912, Britain and Norway launched rival expeditions to the South Pole. Robert F. Scott's team from Britain hauled excessive gear, including luxuries and fine tableware, while the Norwegians, led by Roald Amundsen, traveled lean and fast. Amundsen reached the Pole and returned safely. Scott's sledges, weighed down by vanity, resulted in the death of his entire team.

The next two stories reveal a quieter danger: how clinging tightly to the dead weight of past successes can sink one's future prosperity.

1975—Kodak and the Digital Wave [18]

During the mid-1990's, The Eastman Kodak Company was the fourth-most-valuable global brand, known for their film photography products and their "Kodak Moment" advertising campaign. Unbeknownst to most, this once mighty company actually invented the first digital camera in 1975. But, they buried it under loyalty to their film business, afraid the digital camera would cannibalize its core revenue source.

By clinging to the outdated strip film model, Kodak missed the digital shift and lost out to competitors like Canon and Sony. The company ultimately filed for bankruptcy in 2012 because they chose not to innovate, and instead continued to carry the dead weight of their past successes.

2014—Blockbuster Brick-and-Mortar [19]

Blockbuster was a powerhouse supplier of rental Video Home System tapes for viewing movies at home with a Video Cassette Recorder. At its peak in 2004, Blockbuster had more than 9,000 retail stores globally. Its arch-rival, Netflix, ten years after its inception, introduced streaming services in 2007. Despite new advances in technology, Blockbuster clung to its retail roots and refused to shed the physical weight, in this case, store fronts, of their past success. As a consequence, Blockbuster filed for bankruptcy in 2010 and closed all of their corporate owned stores by 2014.

Each story above shares the same warning: What you cling to can cost you the summit, the prize, and even survival.

In today's world, we bury ourselves in excess that drags us down: overeating, credit card debt, addictions, fast fashion, and piles of possessions. The load we carry steals our focus, drains our energy, and keeps us from what truly matters.

But not all heaviness comes from tangible things. Sometimes the extra weight comes from the company we keep, crew members who no longer row in the same direction or who quietly pull us off course. Releasing those ties isn't heartless; it's how a ship stays seaworthy. When you travel with those who help lift your sails instead of puncturing them, your voyage lightens, and the wind returns to your favor.

Letting go is not loss; it is the clearing of the deck, making space for the journey ahead.

. . .

The bus to the North Rim will leave in two minutes.

Your moment to experience the majesty of the Grand Canyon is just within your reach.

But, you must unload the dead weight from your pack, or else this opportunity will vanish from the horizon!

Out goes the mattress pad.

The water filtration kit, ice cleats, and excrement shovel all get the boot. Even the park's website insists none of it is necessary . . . though you wisely keep the toilet paper.

Every ounce you leave behind helps to lighten your load.
Your backpack is still too heavy! You only have one minute before the bus leaves!

Out goes the bear spray (Cliff says you don't need it). Say goodbye to three days of clothes. Empty one liter of water. After all, you have more water than you could possibly consume. You debate about the bottle of bourbon, but decide it stays!

Now . . . your pack is finally ready. Cliff gives you a high-five, and the bus driver urgently waves for you to board. Immediately!

You hoist the much lighter pack onto your back and board your bus to the North Rim. Through the double doors and up the three steps, you meet the driver face-to-face.

He looks at you mischievously and says, "Glad you could make it." And then he gives you a card.

At first you think it is a ticket for the ride. It isn't until you are seated that you realize it is a handwritten note marked by the smudge of a coffee ring. It reads,

**"What you release will not diminish you; it will make
you light enough to rise. Set your sights on the open water;
the lighter you travel, the farther you'll sail."**

During the ride you find your treasured notebook, trace the words "Aude Volāre" with the tip of your index finger and leaf through the pages reminiscing on your previous journeys and lessons learned. The notebook has already become a powerful source, and you add this note to the collection.

As the bus rolls northward, you think about all the extra weight you unloaded. Do you regret any of it? No, unless you need to protect yourself with the excrement shovel from a rare bear wearing your ice cleats and sleeping on your mattress pad! Otherwise, you'll be just fine, and far more free.

You give Cliff a broad smile and say with a playful jab, "Moment of truth. Hope you brought your A-game!"

PROPELLER PLAN Eliminate Deadweight

Dead weight isn't always obvious. Sometimes it's the clutter that surrounds you, and other times it's the beliefs, roles, or regrets you've carried long past their purpose. These things may have once served you, but if they're now slowing your stride, they're costing you the very journey they once helped you begin. Moving forward requires traveling lighter.

Important considerations include:

1. **Take Inventory.** What are you currently carrying (physical, mental, or emotional) that feels heavy rather than helpful?

2. **Revisit the Purpose.** Did these things once serve a purpose? Do they still serve one now?

3. **Face Fear.** What fears come up when you imagine setting them down?

4. **Imagine Freedom.** If you released them, what new possibilities or paths might open?

5. **Invite Support.** Who or what could walk alongside you to help you lighten your load as you move forward?

Draw two columns and label them "Keeps Me Afloat" and "Pulls Me Under." Under the appropriate column heading, list present commitments, habits, possessions, thoughts, and relationships. This simple exercise reveals where you may need to cut the anchor. With this clearer view, return to the questions above and choose actions that lift you (body, mind, and spirit) so you can sail full speed ahead.

〰〰〰

CHOOSE-YOUR-CURRENT

Standing to exit the bus, you realize there is a message on the back of the note. The coffee ring smudge has bled through to the back of the paper. The note reads,

"With a lighter pack, you now carry the strength to chart new **courses with ease. Ahe**ad, two choices await, trust yourself **to follow the on**e that carries you forward."

Choice One

Cross the Golden Gate Bridge into the pulse of San Francisco's Global Software Conference, where every handshake is a compass, and new crewmates await to guide your course through the currents of connection.

FIND CHAPTER 12: CREWMATES • PAGE 119

Choice Two

Drive north from Seattle to Whistler with your mother for an art retreat. Along winding mountain roads and quiet studio hours, you realize she is the hidden rudder steering this current.

FIND CHAPTER 14: UNEXPECTED ALLY • PAGE 137

As you step off the bus, you notice a steaming mug of coffee in the driver's cup holder, and a compass rose key chain dangling from the ignition. Glancing back over your shoulder, the driver gives you a quick wink before pulling away.

CHAPTER 11

Recharge Your Battery

Create boundaries with yourself,
outline when or how you budget in for self-care.
ADITHI J.

SEPTEMBER, IVY HOME
KANSAS CITY, MISSOURI, U.S.A.
39.1°N, 94.6°W

Staring at yourself in the mirror, you look like you have been awake since 4 a.m. You were hoping to look sharp for your Professional Development Workshop tonight, but your unwashed hair, and growing zit make it impossible for you to feel like you are on your A-game.

Perhaps a caffeine jolt would do you some good. Opening the cupboard in your tiny u-shaped kitchen, you pull out the coffee to see the last two beans at the bottom of the bag, far from enough to make a cup of coffee. A flash of contempt for your partner twists through you as you fling the nearly empty coffee bag out of desperation and the lone beans fly toward the ceiling.

"How can they possibly leave a bag with just two beans?" you groan silently.

Unsure of what to do next, you hoist yourself onto the kitchen counter and survey the house renovation mess before you. You hold your breath and your blood pressure rises. Five months ago you moved to Kansas City with your partner, secured new jobs, and bought an old 1970's townhouse in dire need of a face lift.

Having read copious amounts of real estate investment books, you felt this was the best way to make money and you quickly launched into the renovation of this tired wreck with "good bones," as they say. You mistakenly believed you could quickly flip the house and sell it for a profit as seen on TV. But instead, every little bit is now driving you crazy: the drywall dust, power tool cords, tiny screws, dirty paint brushes, and plastic bags full of unknown pieces and parts. This dream of yours is now demanding more of your time and money than you have to give.

In fact, you are out of money; your credit cards are maxed. Now there is an insane need to finish the renovation and sell the townhouse to recoup your investment. That's why you set your alarm for 4 a.m., to try to paint the half-dark living room before the light of day and before your day job.

Your thoughts continue to whirl, and you think about the second of three payments due for a software certification you're trying to obtain. Initially, you thought the online class was a good idea as a "resumé builder," but the fact is, you don't have the money for the second payment and you don't have the time to complete the course.

Your thoughts are interrupted when you see your dog squat and poop on the brand-new carpet.

"Ho-ly CRAP! Seriously!"

You jump to the floor from your seat on the kitchen counter and stare at the offending waste. You glance at your watch. You're late!

"The dog just pooped on the new carpet," you yell, hoping your voice carries up the stairway!

No answer from your partner.

Time is ticking and you need to leave for your professional development event now. There is no time to clean up the mess. Seething, it would be nice if your partner took responsibility for once.

Again, you yell up the stairway, "The dog poooooooped on the carpet!"

Echoing from the upstairs hallway your partner responds, "Why don't you clean it up?"

You scream, "I've got to go!"

And with that, you stomp out the front door and slam it behind you, trapping your pant leg and knocking over the plant stand, dirt sent flying like shrapnel.

The neighbors can hear you curse from frustration a hundred yards away.

. . .

In 1998, there was a famous "Chocolate and Radish Experiment" conducted by the psychologist Roy Baumeister.[20] The purpose of the study was to test the depletion of the will to continue.

During the study, a group of participants were seated in a room before a tempting display of freshly baked chocolate chip cookies, but were told they couldn't have any. Instead, they were offered pungent radishes. A second group was given the cookies to eat.

To punctuate the test of "willpower depletion" or the "power to move forward," both groups were given a series of "unsolvable" puzzles. At the same time, they were given either the radishes or the chocolate chip cookies to eat while working on the puzzles.

Interestingly, the radish group made far fewer attempts and devoted less than half their time to solving the puzzles as compared to the cookie-eating participants.

When I heard about this experiment, it made a huge impact on me, and I started taking notice in my own life when my personal figurative battery was nearing empty. "Eating radishes" in real life might look like studying for an exam at great lengths with no breaks, caregiving for a sick family member for days on end, wakeful nights with a newborn child, preparing for an Ironman race, or even just limiting breaks because you feel like you don't deserve them! All of these moments can easily stymie your will to power forward and end in burn out.

Using our "lost at sea" analogy, burnout is the result of rowing, rowing, rowing your boat and never giving yourself a break to refresh, enjoy the scenery, take account of where you are and where you are going, or savor new sights.

Living in an endless cycle of difficult tasks results in emotional depletion, chronic fatigue, and disengagement, as displayed by the radish group. Contrastingly, like the chocolate chip cookie group, if you take the time to refresh, you are energized to power forward.

There is a current trend of "we can do hard things." Of course we can. I see my students manage a full class load, full-time career, demanding family responsibilities, and everything in between.

The radish and chocolate chip cookie experiment asks us to take notice when we are "eating too many radishes," living with too much stress and depleting our willpower to continue. If we can notice when our battery is getting low, before giving up and throwing a fit, then we can actively search for ways to recharge.

A taste of delight restores the strength to endure.

During my own college final exams, my car broke down and I didn't have the money to fix it. I was tired, had endless upcoming project deadlines, and the car repairs broke me. I was at the end of my rope and remember falling to the ground and screaming at the top of my lungs out of desperation.

Do you think my reaction would have been different if I had been well-rested and surrounded by supportive friends? I think so! Do you think I might have had the bandwidth to search for a solution to my problem rather than giving up? I think so.

Since I learned about the account of the radishes and chocolate chip cookies, I have grown more adept at measuring my stress level and proactively adding "chocolate chip cookie moments" to my life. When I can't stop to recharge, I try to pause what I am doing, take a deep breath, and figure out when and where I might be able to plug in. Scheduling a future break can help buy time before you lose your willpower to move forward.

Reserves of willpower are renewed in moments of joy.

Yes, reserves of willpower are renewed in moments of joy. But, let's also consider that too much of a good thing can be a bad thing. A dozen chocolate chip cookies? That's a sugar coma waiting to happen.

We live in a world that celebrates both grit and indulgence. "We can do hard things," we tell ourselves, while also whispering "We deserve this." Both are true, until one tips the scales and throws us off balance.

Overindulgence, masked as self-care, can be draining.

Overcharging one's battery may look like: buying luxury items on a maxed-out credit card, inhaling a week's worth of sugar and salt in one sitting, binge-watching shows alone until the sun comes up, or scrolling endlessly through other people's lives while neglecting our own. While indulgence may offer comfort in the moment, too much can leave you feeling worse off.

Undercharging our battery can look like saying yes to everyone but yourself, running on caffeine and obligation, skipping meals, sleep, and silence. Working without rest, giving without renewal, and mistaking busyness for purpose will run your battery dangerously low.

Pausing to charge your battery doesn't slow you down, it brings you back to life. Rest renews focus, fuels creativity, and gives you the power to move forward.

• • •

You yank your pant leg out of the doorway, race to your car, and drive to the professional gathering like a bat out of hell. Clean up will have to wait. Exhaustion and exasperation cloud your sight, and you wonder why you're even bothering to attend, except that you've been wanting to meet some new friends.

You surf through the upscale BBQ smokehouse restaurant filled with overly chipper, animated professionals, grab a drink, and find a corner to sulk by yourself. This is not how you envisioned introducing yourself to the up-and-comers of your new city.

A mid-career professional notes your cloud of despair, casts a broad smile, and takes a seat next to you. Her nametag says, "HELLO, my name is NORA."

She runs her fingers down her long braids and says, "It looks like you've had better days. How are you? Really?"

You had heard people from Kansas City were "salt of the earth." Case in point, Nora's friendliness and sincerity disarm you immediately. You look down and turn your glass in your hands, and the words start pouring out of your mouth.

You tell her about the new move, new job, buying and renovating a townhouse, a partner who doesn't take responsibility, lack of sleep, lack of money, and about trying so hard to develop yourself professionally, but being too exhausted to do so. Plus, the dog pooped on your carpet, and you've got to re-pot your money tree!

Nora once again smiles broadly and knowingly. "Oh, I've been there. Sometimes too many hard things happen all at once.

"Your personal battery is dead," she continues.

Then she asks a pointed question, "When was the last time you took a break, gave yourself grace, and did something to recharge?"

You stare at her blankly. You honestly can't remember the last time you did something for yourself.

Nora quotes, "A small treat can fuel big resilience."

"For example," she continues, "adventure hikers who scale mountains, will often trek a difficult hike up and then return to where they started at base camp for scheduled rest."

Adding one more point, Nora says, "There is also a run-walk-run method for completing foot races where the runners run for a few minutes and then walk for one minute. The walking gives their body a rest allowing them to complete the race. This method has a 98 percent success rate and is nearly injury-free."

This makes sense to you, and you realize that you've been running nonstop. Case in point, getting up at four o'clock this morning to paint, followed by a long day at work, a disastrous segue home, plus trying to sneak in some professional development. Add to that: new job, new house, new relationship, hard, hard, hard!

It's no wonder you haven't been at your best and now you have a relationship mess to clean up, along with the plant dirt and dog poop.

Nora is right, you need to find ways to refresh and renew—now!

Willpower, like any muscle in the body, can develop with use, and similarly, it can strain and tear with overuse.

Continuing, Nora looks at you squarely and says, "Instead of having a drink here by yourself, why don't you go home and have a conversation with your partner about intentionally creating moments of refreshment and identifying what that looks like for you?"

Winking, she says, "I'll be here next week and want to hear an update! Deal?" She extends her hand. Your hand meets hers and you shake on it. "Deal," you respond. When Nora stands to leave, she slips a folded cocktail napkin into your hand.

Opening the napkin you see a looping handwritten message that says,

"Discipline moves you forward, but delight keeps you alive. Choose both, and you'll flourish on the voyage."

You notice a printed logo on the napkin. It's not the BBQ joint's logo, but a compass rose. Suddenly, you feel the strength to return home, clean up your messes, have the tough conversation, and find a way to recharge your battery.

PROPELLER PLAN Charge Your Battery

When you intentionally choose renewal, you'll uncover the secret to staying afloat. Small joys are not indulgences, but lifelines—the breath of wind that fills your sails when the seas grow heavy!

Give yourself permission to pause. Resilience is sustained by balancing endurance with rest.

It is important to learn to proactively read the level of your personal battery. This is an internal gauge of your patience and willpower. The earlier you can detect when your battery is low, the more proactively you can schedule time to restore. Let's take a reading of your figurative battery . . .

1. **Identify Your Energy Leaks.** What recurring events in your life drain you? Protect your power source.

2. **Notice the Warning Signs.** What are your telltale signs that your personal battery is getting low?

3. **Know What Recharges You.** What actions can you take to refuel?

4. **Communicate What You Need.** Next time you find your battery low, how will you handle it, and how will you communicate your needs with yourself and to those around you?

Look ahead at your week and choose one moment each day for something restorative: a walk, a favorite song, a nap, or a video call with a dear friend in another city. Identify the points in your routine where your willpower usually dips. Place your "strength breaks" there, so you refuel before running aground.

At day's end, ask yourself: did I only do hard things, or did I also find moments of renewal? Adjust tomorrow's course to include both.

CHOOSE-YOUR-CURRENT

After seeing the compass rose image, you turn the napkin over and find another message. It's an invitation to find much needed refreshment and recharge your battery. You have two choices.

Choice One

Slip beneath Roatán's sunlit waves, where fear loosens its grip the moment you let a guiding hand lead you through the depths.

FIND CHAPTER 13: FIGHT, FLIGHT, OR FLOAT • PAGE 127

Choice Two

Journey from Seattle to Whistler with your mother for an art retreat. Amid mountain passes and paint-streaked canvases, you finally recognize that her steady rudder is your guiding light.

FIND CHAPTER 14: UNEXPECTED ALLY • PAGE 137

Taking your treasured notebook out of your backpack, you flatten the napkin between two pages. You are struck by this powerful moment and feel the ever watchful eye of your Grandfather Muse.

SECTION VI

Guiding Lights

ALLIES, MENTORS AND MESSAGES THAT STEER YOU

CHAPTER 12

Crewmates

There is not always one direct path … connections are super important to have in any field; make, maintain and expand connections.
TEJAH B.

**OCTOBER, MOSCONE CENTER
SAN FRANCISCO, CALIFORNIA U.S.A.
37.8°N, 122.4°W**

It is a colorful mid-October day, and you are on a plane to San Francisco for your first "real" business trip to attend the Global Software Conference. To fit the part, you have a professional haircut and are dressed in your new black suit and (far too expensive) painful shoes. Even though you are nervous, you are excited to see the city and eat expensive meals on your company's dime! You are even hoping for a bit of personal time so you can see the Golden Gate Bridge and wet your blistered feet in the Pacific Ocean.

A seasoned veteran of your firm is traveling with you, and he is expected to mentor you about the art of striking up conversations as business development with prospective clients. Ironically, he is a man of few words and so far, he hasn't said anything to you. Walking toward the opening dinner reception, your supposed 'mentor' quips,

"We should probably split up so we can meet people," and he stalks off in the opposite direction.

Startled and horrified, you scan the sea of attendees seated at large round tables. It appears you are the youngest professional in attendance and probably the least experienced. You take a deep breath and say silently to yourself, "Here it goes." Figuratively, you dive into the crowd, almost expecting the non-existent water to splash your face.

A round table to your right, flanked with eleven middle aged men, has one open seat that could have your name on it. They are talking amongst each other, but you quietly interrupt the conversation next to the open chair to ask if it is taken. An older 'techie' gentleman with funky glasses says, "I don't think so." He quickly turns back to his discussion. You take a seat, pinned between a din of conversation among software engineers.

As you dine on rice pilaf (a staple at any conference dinner), you wonder how you will strike up a conversation. Awkwardness overcomes your body, and you want to run and hide in your lavish hotel room. Swimming in uncomfortable silence, and with nothing to lose, you decide to lean into your unrefined social skills. You chuckle, noting the weirdness of the situation.

You decide to make a bet with yourself, *I bet I can get this entire table of executives talking with me before dinner is over.* Your former teachers might say you are betting against the odds, nevertheless, you are eager to prove you can do it.

As conversation lulls, you seize the moment. "Gentlemen, I have a question. Since we're at a software conference . . ."

Your voice trembles, but you push through. "What do you see as the most transformative tech trend in the next five years, and how will it shape our industry?"

. . .

"When transitioning from a student to developing a successful career . . . networking and building professional relationships is especially challenging for introverted individuals."

STELLA L.

Networking isn't about forcing connections, it's about letting conversations carry you into new waters. When you approach others with curiosity and authenticity, you'll find that doors open more easily. Each person you meet may hold a key insight, an unseen opportunity, or a friendship that strengthens your voyage.

The word "networking" is overused, and the thought of it can invoke unease. Let's reframe the idea and think of it as a time to

"Grow Your Professional Circle."

Can you imagine the difference in the outcome if you entered a room thinking, I look forward to growing my circle.

Instead of thinking, I feel so intimidated, bored, unenthused, or put off by this crowd, try walking into your next event with a sense of curiosity and possibility to Grow Your Professional Circle. After all, you might just meet someone who could positively change the direction of your story.

If anxiety rises, remember, anxiety isn't something to conquer, but to understand. Let it be the quiet companion that reminds you you're human, and **courage doesn't mean calm, it means showing up.** Even the best sailors feel apprehension against the ocean's waves.

Courage begins with one breath. Slow your breathing, remind yourself you're here to learn, and let curiosity guide your conversation.

You may not be looking for a job right now, but three in five people are, according to LinkedIn Pressroom 2025.[21] Here's a startling networking statistic. According to a 2025 LinkedIn article, "From 70 to 85 percent of jobs are filled through networking. Meanwhile, online job *applications have an average success rate of about 2 percent!"* [22]

That means 98 percent of online cold applications end up in a virtual black hole!

The data confirms your suspicions, doesn't it? Those of us who have applied to jobs online without a connection already know that it can feel hopeless. The reason most "cold" applications go nowhere is because of the overwhelming volume of applications, applicant tracking software systems, and AI recruiting tools.

Hiring relies on trust, so it's no wonder most jobs are filled through referrals, networking, and internal recommendations. Recruiters naturally prioritize someone who's been introduced by an employee or trusted colleague over an anonymous résumé from the internet. The key to finding your next role is to continuously grow your professional connections. You never know when these contacts could help bridge your next chapter!

A strong referral can catapult your résumé past the recruiting black hole . . . and land it directly on a decision-maker's desk. Conversations with new people can be turning points, uncovering opportunities hidden just beyond your view.

. . .

Back at the dinner table, your question about tech trends in five years launches the executives into deep debate. Thus, you not only win your own bet, but you learn a few things. With a single question, you are able to make new connections and secure business meetings with a return trip to San Francisco already on the books.

In this moment, you realize networking isn't about handing out business cards; it's about sparking conversations that build trust, curiosity, and shared respect. These connections can open doors no cold application ever could.

The older "techie" gentleman with the funky glasses scribbles on a piece of paper torn from a legal pad and slides it across the table to you, his eyes twinkling with something between mischief and mentorship. He doesn't elaborate, just taps the corner of the paper like it holds a map only you can read.

Shaking your hand, he says that he looks forward to seeing you again soon. With that he heads toward the exit to find the vendor hall.

When he's gone, you study the message written on the lined yellow paper,

**"Grow your circle and your course expands.
Every new connection charts an untraveled current,
one that may carry you to unimagined shores."**

Not only did you prevail in your bet and gain new connections, but you learned the value of growing your professional circle. What began as a single question at the dinner table turned into a genuine exchange and over time turned into meaningful client relationships, future job offers, and personal growth through relationship building.

The resulting connections would have never happened if you had run back to the safety of your hotel room instead of choosing to sit at a table of strangers . . . or shall we say, possible future colleagues, mentors, and friends. Eventually, because of the breadth of your connections you are able to create a connecting web of professional support that reaches beyond borders. Yes, you are growing your circle.

PROPELLER PLAN Grow Your Circle

"Growing Your Professional Circle" isn't about inserting yourself into every room or conversation, it's about stepping in with curiosity, easing your own anxiety with a steady breath, and allowing authentic connections to unfold. Each genuine exchange expands your circle and steers you closer to opportunities you could never reach alone.

Consider these tips:

1. Connect through Curiosity. Start with curiosity and prepare at least three open-ended questions you can use as conversation starters that invite people to share their experiences and ideas with you. Reach Out. Write down the names of five people you haven't connected with in a while. Reach out with a genuine note to check in.

2. Put Yourself in the Path. Attend one professional event, club, or gathering this month that interests you, and commit to starting at least one thoughtful and engaging conversation.

3. Reflect and Reconnect. After each interaction, jot down one thing you learned and one way you could follow up.

4. Secure the Current of Connection. Choose one person to schedule a follow-up coffee, call, or meeting—keeping the current of connection alive.

Growing your circle is about cultivating real connections that carry you further than you could travel alone. Once you gather your crew, you can begin charting a course toward new horizons.

CHOOSE-YOUR-CURRENT

Opening the folded note, you realize there is another message you had missed before.

> **"Conversations are** currents, you never know which
> **one will carry you farther** than you dreamed. To grow,
> **you must set** your sail toward learning.

Two harbors await, which will you choose?"

Choice One

Take the helm of a valuable deal in Buenos Aires, guiding your team through uncharted waters, where true success is measured not by the pitch alone but by following up with gratitude.

FIND CHAPTER 15: FOLLOW-UP • PAGE 149

Choice Two

Go to St. Vincent to help restore the natural habitat of the Windward Islands. Here, you learn that wealth isn't measured in minutes or money, but in generosity, gratitude, and the gentle rhythm of community.

FIND CHAPTER 16: EPIC VOYAGE • PAGE 155

There is a simple compass rose sketched in pen on the corner of the note, partially covered by a coffee ring. You turn the paper so the arrow points north. Smiling, you place it for safekeeping between two pages of your weathered notebook.

To no one in particular, you exhale a sigh of relief and say, "I am going to put my feet in the Pacific Ocean."

CHAPTER 13

Fight, Flight, or Float

There is a need for guidance and direction.
DEAGO D.

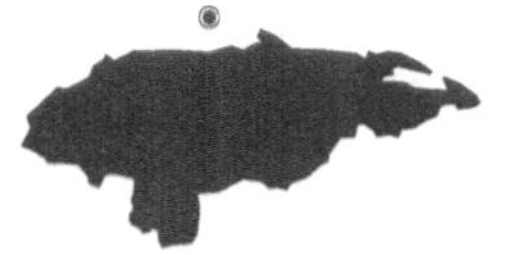

**FEBRUARY, WEST BAY
ROATÁN, HONDURAS
16.3°N, 86.5°W**

Over the sound of the slapping green ocean waves, you hear your sun-kissed dive instructor say,

"Just fall backward into the water."

You are precariously propped on the edge of the small dive boat with a heavy air tank on your back. Your body freezes, and your brain kicks into high gear with racing thoughts,

I don't dive! I don't put my head under the water.

I don't like water in my ears or my eyes!

What am I doing here? Shouldn't I be hanging out at the cabana with a piña colada in my hand?

You've been invited to your school friend's family bungalow on the island of Roatán off the coast of Honduras. The island may be small, only thirty-seven miles long and less than five miles across, but it boasts a sun-drenched population of 100,000, about half of whom are expats seeking sand, ocean, and better living, much like your friend's family.

You find a low-cost connecting flight through Houston which makes the entire trip affordable. Roatán is a scuba diver's paradise, you come to understand, home to the second-largest barrier reef in the world—second only to the Great Barrier Reef off the coast of Australia.

Your friends are surprised that you are hesitant to scuba dive, not knowing this is one of your greatest fears! Your visceral reactions to diving have been deeply seeded in the fibers of your being since your early interactions with water. You love being ON the water, NOT IN the water.

You learned to swim on the brink of hypothermia in the frozen tundra, where the air was fifty degrees and the water even colder. You can confirm, it was not "character building."

Despite trauma that still feels very real, you are being dragged into getting SCUBA certified because, according to your friends, you can't miss the unexplored underwater world. Plus, it might be time to face your fears. Most importantly, your Zen divemaster assures you they will be by your side the entire time. With an earnest look, you know they mean it.

During dive certification, you practice every aquatic nightmare imaginable: flooding your mask, running out of oxygen, sharing air with your so-called "dive buddy," and performing a "controlled" emergency ascent that feels anything but controlled. Each scenario presses hard against your inner panic button, exasperated of course, by the *Jaws* soundtrack on repeat in your head.

You always vowed that you would never dive into water, and you haven't . . . until now, when the divemaster instructs, "Just fall backward into the ocean." The tone of their voice and steady presence make you feel . . . prepared?

• • •

Instructors, therapists, professors, teachers, trainers, mentors, coaches, and guides are imbued with wisdom from their own journeys. Having taken the figurative leap off the ship, they swam against currents, braved stormy seas, prepared their vessels, and steered their voyages through which they gained their wisdom.

There are many examples of mentor-mentee relationships where the student had to overcome a fear to achieve their vision or passion.

Take for example:

Nelson Mandela & Walter Sisulu[23]

As a young lawyer entering the fight against apartheid in South Africa, Nelson Mandela feared the consequences of political defiance—retaliation, violence, and imprisonment. Walter Sisulu, a seasoned activist, mentored Mandela, teaching him patience, strategy, and resilience, helping him see resistance as a moral calling worth the fight. That guidance prepared Mandela to endure twenty-seven years in prison and later serve as the first Black president of South Africa.

Helen Keller & Anne Sullivan[24]

Blind and deaf from a young age, Helen Keller's fear of isolation seemed insurmountable. Anne Sullivan, her teacher and mentor who was also blind, patiently helped Keller find language through human touch. I'll never forget the dramatic scene from the movie The Miracle Worker where Anne taught Helen to say the word "water" while using an outdoor pump. With Sullivan's guidance, Keller transformed her fear into confidence, becoming a world-renowned author and activist for people with disabilities.

Dr. Martin Luther King, Jr. & Benjamin Mays [25]

As a seminary student, Martin Luther King, Jr. wrestled with leading during the 1950s and 1960s, a dangerous time of racial inequality in the United States. Benjamin Mays, president of Morehouse College, became King's mentor, urging him to see leadership as a calling, not a burden. Mays' influence shaped King's courage to lead the Civil Rights Movement in the U.S.

When I first meet my students at Georgia State University, many carry the invisible weight of fear: fear of failure, judgment, and not being enough. But as the months pass, courage begins to surface. You can see it in their posture, their laughter, the light in their eyes. My role as professor, guiding these students through their transformation is like watching the tide rise, quiet, powerful, unstoppable.

I met Juan when he was a junior in college, at that time he was terrified to speak in front of even the smallest audience. Yet his love for people and his authentic smile were contagious. I encouraged him to take on a leadership role among his peers and to strengthen his presentation skills. We began consistent mentoring with weekly group and individual coaching sessions, sharpening his skills by exposing him to public speaking opportunities.

After a year, Juan became the president of an influential student club. He also won awards for his presentation skills, and now speaks confidently to groups of more than 100 students. He openly shares about his early fears, inspiring others to embrace their own potential. It's stories like Juan's that make mentoring so rewarding.

It's important to remember that finding a mentor who can guide you in every area of life is rare, and that's okay. In my own experience, mentors often shine in one specific area. You may end up with a diverse network of individuals in your mastermind community, each bringing a unique perspective to their role: a coach, counselor, financial advisor, relationship confidant, or spiritual guide. After all, you wouldn't necessarily want your financial advisor giving you relation-ship advice, or your spiritual guide offering athletic tips!

As you grow, you'll notice that some mentors come and go, while others remain for a lifetime. The key is to stay open to finding and building your mastermind community. And remember, your guides are often found where you least expect them.

Each of the aforementioned examples reminds us of a timeless truth: fear rarely disappears on its own. It is through the steady presence of a mentor that fear is transformed into focus, weakness into strength, and hesitation into bold action. These examples show us that no one navigates uncharted waters alone, we rise on the shoulders of those who guide us.

. . .

"Just fall backward into the ocean," rings through your ears.

You take a deep breath, press your regulator and goggles firmly against your face, and fall backward, somersaulting through the clearest, bluest ocean water that you have ever seen. You are giddy that you took the plunge. Inexplicable joy and weightless peace ripple through your core.

Then you hear the sound of your exhale bubbles push through the regulator with a loud gurgle. The steep coral cliffs spiral and blur to depths you haven't seen before. You grow dizzy, your heart pounds hard, and you suck on your regulator trying to pull every molecule of air out of the tank. The slow, not-so-subtle, two-note *dun-dun* of the *Jaws* theme starts playing in your head.

Duuun-dun . . . duuun-dun . . . duuun-dun duuun-dun duuun-dun.

You feel like you can't catch a breath. Your heart pounds harder, and panic sets in. Despite being told to stay underwater, you kick your fins as hard as you can to break through the surface for air.

Removing the regulator you squall, "I can't do this, I can't do this, I can't do this!"

Your instructor slowly crests the surface, looks you in your masked eyes, and uses his hand to motion the meditative rhythm of the slow, slow inhale . . . and slow, slow exhale.

He points to your head and says, "Your fear is only here. If you can master your mind, you can master diving."

You digest that concept and then respond thoughtfully, "Do you think I can actually calm my mind and body enough to face my greatest fear?"

The divemaster calmly muses, *"You have practiced for every emergency scenario; you are ready from a textbook standpoint. Now, you need to do the much deeper and harder emotional work to face your fear. This is done little by little, not in one giant leap."*

The Zen divemaster continues a gentle command, *"Breathe at my meditative pace and let's see if you can stay underwater for two seconds longer than before."*

You admire this powerful advice! Of course, you can stay underwater for two more seconds.

In fact, it is 30 long seconds before you claw for the surface again. That afternoon the zen divemaster stays by your side as you practice your underwater dive. You finally catch the rhythm of meditative breathing, and you give the nod that you are ready. You know the seriousness of what it means when you nod for "go time."

The divemaster, your friends, and you (yes, you) descend to 60 feet below the surface of the ocean. Much like a conductor of a symphony, the divemaster waves his hand back and forth to the timing of the slow, slow, meditative breaths.

You land on the sandy bottom of the ocean and the iridescent coral walls tower high above your mask. You feel your finned foot reach the sand, likening it to the landing of Neil Armstrong on the moon. His famed "one small step" words ring in your head. Although, this is certainly a GIANT STEP for you!

As if on cue, you are confronted with your SECOND greatest

fear! In the distance, you see a larger-than-life SHARK swimming directly toward you.

You lock eyes with its beady pupils.

Duuun-dun…duuun-dun…duuun-dun duuun-dun duuun-dun.

Consciously, you keep your breathing slow and rhythmic. The fierce fish continues swimming toward you until suddenly, it turns and swims unbothered away from you into the murky depths in search of its real prey.

You're stunned.

You have just come nose-to-nose with another one of your greatest fears, and somehow it wasn't nearly as dramatic as you expected. In the end, your fears were softened into courage by breathwork, and guided by trust in the mentor beside you.

Though extraordinarily difficult, confronting this diving experience is a moment of inexplicable healing for you.

At the Bananarama Dive Shop, you put away your gear and share stories with the fellow divers about your thrilling shark encounter. The Zen divemaster gives you a wise and congratulatory nod, "You did it. I'm so proud of you. My guidance didn't erase your fear, it showed you how to move with it, one breath at a time."

The divemaster writes the details of the dive in your logbook. You smile and are overcome with a calm sense of satisfaction. When your log is returned, you notice another piece of paper sticking out between the pages of the dive book.

The note says,

"The shark passed and so did the terror you expected.
What remains is trust.
A guide's presence turns fear into focus,
silence into strength,
and strength into the confidence
to swim on your own."

The note is written on Bananarama stationary. You laugh out loud when you see that your Zen divemaster has drawn a figure of a shark and diver swimming around the compass rose. You remember the moment you came face to face with the shark and now pause to revel in the sense of relief, courage, and personal growth you feel.

PROPELLER PLAN Tackle Fear with a Guide

Fear isn't always a storm; it can be a quiet undercurrent. When you lean on a supportive guide, you learn how to steady your breath, and in time, you discover the strength to navigate on your own. Trust lightens the weight of fear, giving you buoyancy to rise above it.

Take a moment to consider these key points.

1. **Name Your Fear.** Write down one fear that keeps surfacing in your life or career.

2. **Choose Your Guide.** Identify a mentor, coach, or peer you trust to help you face that fear. Remember, you may need a network of guides to support your growth.

3. **Breathe.** The next time you feel anxious, pause to take three slow breaths, reminding yourself that calm creates clarity.

4. **Practice Swimming Solo.** Choose one small step you can take alone, proving to yourself that you can carry forward the strength you've gained.

Fear may surface in unexpected ways, but with the guidance of a trusted mentor, it can be transformed into focus and strength, and eventually, the courage to stand on your own.

CHOOSE-YOUR-CURRENT

On the back of the note, another message reads,

**"Having stood before your fear, the horizon
opens to test your spirit once more.
Two adventures lie ahead,
only you can choose which tide to follow."**

Choice One

Manage a high stakes deal in Argentina's capital city, guiding your team through uncharted waters, where true success is measured not by the pitch alone but by the diligence of following up.

FIND CHAPTER 15: FOLLOW-UP • PAGE 149

Choice Two

Launch your new business on Boston's historic School Street, where the echoes of past ventures spark new beginnings, and you realize true courage is in the ability to pivot when the path no longer fits your purpose.

FIND CHAPTER 17: CHANGING COURSE • PAGE 163

You turn the paper over and once again stare at the logo of the compass rose with the hand drawn shark and diver. Pulling your notebook out of your backpack, you realize the cover of the book is growing more weathered and its contents becoming more dear. You trace the words *"Aude Volāre"* and place the new note in the middle of the book.

You muse, "I am ready for my next adventure!"

CHAPTER 14

Unexpected Ally

The benefits available from colleges are prevalent, but often hard to find or know about without directly being told. Many students don't know what opportunities they should take advantage of.

QUINN H.

**MARCH, ARTIST RETREAT
WHISTLER, BRITISH COLUMBIA, CANADA
50.1°N, 123.0°W**

Sitting on a hard wooden chair, you take in the fragrance of freshly roasted coffee at the original 1971 Starbucks in Seattle's famed Pike's Market. Perched on the edge of the Pacific Ocean, this place always helps you feel centered. Today, you are waiting for your mother who has invited you to drive with her five hours north to Whistler, British Columbia, for a week-long art retreat.

Your relationship with your mother is complicated. It's always seemed she's been competitive with you and held you back despite what her "encouraging" words might say. After careful consideration you accept her invitation, although you are a bit wary. First and foremost, you aren't an artist, but you think it might be a good way to explore Canada, get away from your daily routine, and perhaps grow closer to your mother along the way. You pack your patience and wait at the designated rendezvous point for her arrival.

Five minutes past the top of the hour, your mother sweeps through the entrance and gives you an obligatory hug. The two of you walk in forced conversation to the rental car company and start loading her packed art supplies. The two French easels, oodles of canvases, three tackle boxes of paints, six large-volume books about painting, a large round tube for some unknown reason, and two huge suitcases don't even come close to fitting in the micro-car she rented.

It's like stuffing ten pounds of crap into a five-pound bag.

Whispering to the agent while rolling your eyes, you sneer, "We're going to need an upgrade." Even in the second car, now midsized, her art supplies stick out the windows. It's still too small. Another upgrade. Still no room for your single suitcase.

More eyerolls and another upgrade. You finally end up with the largest car the company has, and you breathe a sigh of relief that your mother is paying for it.

Your mother decides you are the driver, and she is the navigator, but you question this when in the first fifteen minutes on the road she leans her head back and falls asleep. You are quite sure the "sleeping" is to avoid the tension of your unspoken history.

"This might be a really long week," you say to yourself as you scroll to find an early morning drive playlist.

Stopping for gas, your mother wakes up and follows you into the station, judging the nutritional content of each snack you select to buy. "You can't eat that," she quips, "It will make you sick."

"Oh, you shouldn't eat that either. Nor that," she condemns.

You know she's right, but instead you throw an electric glance letting her know to back off. Flinging open the exit door, you stalk back to the huge "land yacht" rental car and wonder if this trip was really a good idea.

After two hours of driving, you arrive at the Canadian border. You and your mother glance at each other in surprise seeing the long lines of vehicles in both directions. Agents in official dark blue uniforms circle each motor vehicle, asking questions of where you've been and where you're going, and even using a mirror to view underneath the cars in search of illegal contraband. The two of you feel as if you are in a covert operation together as you search for your passports.

Once on the other side of the border, your mother turns her whole body toward you from the passenger seat and says,

"Thanks for doing this. I'm not sure I would go without you. I'm glad you're here."

A little trickle of tension starts to melt, and you cast a small smile.

The previously straight path now starts to wind into the Sea-to-Sky Highway. As you round a corner, both of you gasp in unison as the breathtaking expanse of mountains unfold before you. Veering the car to a roadside viewpoint, you park the rental, and the two of you run to the edge of the road to inhale nature's wonder.

Holding her forefinger and thumb from each hand into the air, your mother makes the shape of a square to direct her line of sight. She peers through this human lens with one eye shut. You've seen her do this many times, almost daily for as long as you can remember. This makeshift frame helps her contextualize how she might approach a painting from her current view.

You're curious to know what she is seeing.

She drops one hand, and points to the horizon with the other. She explains the rule of thirds, the contrast of light and dark, and the importance of the foreground for perspective. You've heard all these lessons before, but somehow, right now they feel fresh and new.

"Do you see the snow on top of that peak?" she asks. "What color is that snow?"

You both snicker simultaneously as you realize she's asked you about the color of snow ever since you were five years old on your first pair of skis.

"I know it's not white," you reply proudly!

She raises her hand with her finger pointing toward you.

She continues, "You're right! The color of snow is not what we think. It is light blue, and pink, and lavender, and gray. It's more beautiful, rich, and complex than we are led to believe."

Just like our relationship, you muse silently to yourself.

You look your mother deeply in the eyes and say, "Do you realize you've been teaching me about art all my life?"

Shaking her head, your mother quips, "No, I don't think of it as teaching. It's just life. Just the way I see life."

It dawns on you for the very first time that you've had more than two decades of daily art lessons from your mother. A sudden reverence for your mother's knowledge starts blooming.

How could I have missed that perspective?

The two of you return to the car, and your earlier agitation begins to melt into respect. You may have had a teacher and ally all along and never realized it.

. . .

As with most of the tales recounted in these chapters, this story is rooted in my own experiences. Parent–child ties are the messiest multiple-choice: (a) complicated (b) beautiful (c) stressful (d) all of the above.

Growing up with an artist mother was a quirky experience. Color was the birthplace of beauty; therefore, everything had to be visually perfect, down to the color of the clothes I wore. My mother insisted that I carry a pocket color guide to use when shopping for clothes. Heaven forbid I wore a color that was a shade too light or dark.

Our family vacations were spent in art museums studying the master painters, and our freezer at home was filled with oil paints for safekeeping. My years were filled with practicing the piano and taking lessons from a stern nun while my mother eavesdropped with a listening ear. It's ironic that I nearly failed my required "Music and Art Appreciation" college class because I was bored with the content that I had heard hundreds of times before.

It took me a couple of decades to take a hard look at my bond with my mother, finally seeing her for what she COULD offer and not for her quirky, artistic traits. This wasn't an easy journey, however. It started when I was sent to bedrest after unexpected invasive surgery and my mother quickly came to my aid. It was during my months and months of slow rehabilitation that my relationship blossomed with my artist, teacher, and insightful mother.

One bright fall afternoon, I sat outside, soaking in the sun after surgery. My mother took the opposite end of the couch. It was then that I found the words to thank her for her steady care. It was a powerful moment; tears brimmed in both our eyes. I moved beside her and hugged her. Something between us changed.

The word "mentor" didn't seem quite right to describe my mom's precious role. During the past several years, mentorship has become a buzzword for corporate networking. In reality, mentors are guides who focus on development and offer wisdom, perspective, and advice from their own experiences. A mentor is like a lighthouse: steady, visible, and offering direction.

My relationship with my mother was a bit different from a typical mentor/mentee connection. She was an advocate who stood beside me and backed me up during pivotal moments. Her support was subtly shifting the currents to undergird my journey. Once again using the theme of this content, my mother was like an unseen rudder, propelling me from behind to help me move forward . . . without me even realizing her impact.

No, mentor is not the right word. This time the word that most closely defines my mother's multi-dimensional role is ALLY.

An ally—finally revealed.

Many of life's most profound, unsung allies are hiding in plain sight and whose influence only becomes clear in hindsight. With their words, encouragement, and leading by example, they quietly shape us, guiding us toward a future we can't yet see.

By pausing to reflect on those who have encouraged or stood by our side, we can see that allies are often woven into the fabric of our everyday relationships.

The lesson is simple: the people who shape our future may already be by our side.

. . .

Pulling the rolling art studio on wheels into Whistler, you are greeted by towering mountain peaks punctuated by pine forests that act as a parenthesis to this moment in time. The retreat building looks like a ski lodge constructed of timber; a stone hearth with a roaring fire welcomes you. Warmed with potential, your mother hooks her arm around yours in an unfamiliar gesture suggesting alliance. You're on the same team.

Your mother doesn't waste any time unloading the packed car and touching brush to canvas as if to capture the tide of creativity. You stand at a distance and watch her process in silence, mystified that a few initial jagged lines unfold into beauty from her expert hand.

She then sets up the second French easel and offers you a palette of paints. You squirm and recoil, "I'm not an artist. I only paint as a means of catharsis."

"Maybe you should channel that catharsis with intention," she says wisely, handing you the brush.

Hesitantly, you start sweeping the brush back and forth as your mother barks instruction.

"Stand back. Look closer. View through this mirror. Now the magnifying glass."

Her commands seem harsh, but you realize every great artist

needs someone on their side. Could your mother really be your ally? Lost in thought, your mother instructs, "Keep painting. Now look at your foreground; let the color bounce around. You need a touch of red."

She turns her head back and forth to get a better view; then raises both hands to again put her forefingers and thumbs together as a frame. She looks through her human lens and then says, "Stop!"

She pauses. A vacuum of silence fills the studio. You both walk several paces from the canvas and view it standing side by side.

"It's done," she whispers. "It's a *wow*."

You've never had a compliment like that from your mother and tears nearly come to your eyes. She then states matter-of-factly and with an edge of pride, "You're an artist."

This is a definitive moment for you. Your artist mother has subtly taught you about art since childhood, but you didn't fully recognize it until now. You now see her as an ally; her hidden rudder has been supporting and helping to shift the current in your favor to expose your own true gifts.

"I am an artist." You allow the words to become a reality, simply because your mother can see it in you.

As the day draws to a close, your mother packs up her art supplies. Before she shuts the lid on her tackle box of paints, she hands you a folded piece of sketch paper and gives you a hug. This time it's a bit warmer than her normal frigid clasp.

As your mother strikes up a conversation with another fellow artist, you open the note and read,

"The brightest lights are often the ones we shield our eyes from; turn toward them, and they will guide your way."

Pulling your treasured notebook out of your backpack, you cherish how this book is becoming more weathered with each mile and more dear with each new note.

PROPELLER PLAN Spot Your Ally

Sometimes the allies who shape us most profoundly are already woven into our lives. Their support may be so steady and familiar that we overlook their influence until a moment of clarity reveals the truth.

Consider these points:

1. **Note Your Hidden Influencers.** Write down three people in your life who have quietly influenced your character, habits, or decisions.

2. **Uncover the Lessons.** Identify one quality or action you have unconsciously learned from these individuals you may have overlooked.

3. **Keep an Open Mind.** As you interact with people over the next month, ask yourself, "What can I learn from this person?" Record these new insights. This practice sharpens your ability to recognize guidance in everyday interactions.

4. **Recognize Your Guiding Voices.** Reach out this week with a note, text, or small act of thanks acknowledging your hidden ally's influence. This will strengthen your bond and reveal even more wisdom.

Knowing that allies can hide in plain sight reminds us to value the relationships that have quietly guided us all along. The very constant of these hidden beacons is the reason they often go unnoticed.

**Recognizing who's got your back will
not only bring you gratitude, but also serve as a
guiding light for your voyage ahead.**

✸✸✸

CHOOSE·YOUR·CURRENT

While considering the subtle power of the note from your mother, you turn over the sketch paper and find another written message.

**"The allies you need are already near;
open your eyes, and their light will illuminate
the path toward your next lesson."**

Choice One

Head to St. Vincent as a volunteer and discover that real wealth is not measured in schedules or salaries, but in generosity, gratitude, and belonging.

FIND CHAPTER 16: EPIC VOYAGE • PAGE 155

Choice Two

Launch your dream career on Boston's historic School Street, where the legacy of past ventures stirs fresh ambition, and you discover that real courage isn't turning a blind eye, it's daring to redraw the map when the path no longer serves your purpose.

FIND CHAPTER 17: CHANGING COURSE • PAGE 163

You place the sketch paper between two pages and feel grateful for the hidden, complicated, and beautiful ally your mother has been all along.

With your notebook and backpack in hand, you step outside for a breath of fresh air. Bringing together your forefingers and thumbs, you peer through your frame, taking in the pinnacle view through a lens of hope and excitement for the voyage ahead.

⚓

SECTION VII

Turning Point

TOOLS, FUEL AND COURSE CORRECTIONS

CHAPTER 15

Follow-Up

Following back up with people is something I struggle with.
I meet people, and network with them, but afterwards
I have trouble with how to reach back out.
JENNA T.

DECEMBER, EL FARO
BUENOS AIRES, ARGENTINA
34.6°S, 58.4°W

Between endless meetings you run for a much-needed afternoon coffee break at a café across the street from the iconic skyscraper, *El Faro*, where you're renting an apartment. Most expats simply refer to the towering building as "The Lighthouse." The twin skyscraper complex is conveniently located a short walk from your office in the hub of the city, yet near the water with docks, ferry piers, and a nature reserve not far away. Thus, the Lighthouse name is apropos.

It's been a year since you moved to Buenos Aires for your management job, and the skyline still leaves you breathless. Squinting, you can almost see sparks of energy reflecting off glass and steel. Black and yellow cabs, buses, and scooters grind along the path between your apartment, the coffee shop and your firm.

Sprinting back to your computer at the office, you quicken your pace crossing Avenida del Libertador before the traffic signal changes and you nearly catch your heel on a raised manhole cover. Coffee still intact, you breathe a sigh of relief that you weren't mowed down by the oncoming traffic and that you didn't spill any of the overpriced caffeine fix.

Flashing your employee badge to the security guard, you press the elevator button for the forty-second floor. As you ascend through the clouds, your mind is zooming in lockstep about the complexities of the largest potential sales deal for your division—ever! You are expecting an email update about the business decision, and it had better be good news.

This is an important agreement, and, as the manager of the team, meeting your financial goals rides on winning this contract. A deal of this size has required months of your expertise demonstrating products, answering hundreds of detailed questions, and customizing strategy for the potential client. Your direct manager, Frederico, the Executive Vice President, also has a stake in the game, having invested significant time and travel.

Sitting at your desk, you receive the highly anticipated email that the contract is signed, noting,

"It's time for celebration!"

You ring the bell to signal to your staff and colleagues you've closed the deal, and your team dances with exuberance at the incredible achievement. They call the deal *la ballena*, or *the whale*, because of its size. The lead salesperson is set to earn a commission check befitting the name.

The next morning, Frederico stalks into your office; his face shows obvious disappointment. At first, he doesn't say anything, pacing back and forth on the sunlit carpet, shadows casting from the large plateglass window.

He finally pauses, rests his fingertips on your desk, and leans toward you. His eyes find your pupils and build a tight bridge to your gaze. A single bead of nervous sweat drips down your cheek.

The Executive Vice President says in a low and measured voice, "I've personally worked for nearly a year on that multi-million-dollar deal. I gave my expertise while giving up time that could have been spent on other opportunities. I gave up nights with my family.

"It is worth it financially for our company, and I am happy to help." He stops there and pauses. Continuing, he says, "But your lead salesperson never said, 'Thank you'.

"All I want is a 'thank you' for my efforts and expertise."

With that, your boss threatens, "I will never again refer that employee to another deal!"

Punctuating his last sentence, Frederico turns on his heels, stalks out the door, and slams it behind him.

. . .

Recently, I received a scathing email from a CEO whom I had referred two strong candidates for interviews. His email expressed disappointment that there had been no follow-up from either candidate after their meetings. He took the lack of communication as a RED FLAG and wasn't likely to move forward with either individual.

He said: "We have internal expectations that candidates follow-up within 24 hours of an interview. Prompt and professional follow-up is key, and we typically take lack of follow-up as a sign of either limited interest or a misalignment with our communication expectations."

Ouch! The CEO stuck to his word and didn't hire either individual.

Following up with purpose, and saying thank you with sincerity, demonstrates character, gratitude, and connectedness. In a competitive world, it's not just your performance that sets you apart, it's your intentional follow-up.

You don't need to be a polished speaker or have the most experience to win, you just need to be the one who shows up fully engaged, follows up, and finishes well. Consistency, courtesy, and confidence create ripples that people remember. Your thoughtful follow up might be the very thing that turns a "maybe" into a "yes."

In a world where many forget the final step, purposeful follow-up will help you to stand out and finish strong.

. . .

Once again, in your plush office on the forty-second floor, you are interviewing a candidate for a leadership role on your team. Though you have conducted countless interviews during your career, you still feel that unsettled hope of finding just the right person for the next role.

When the interview ends, the candidate pauses, heartily shakes your hand, and then asks for your business card so they can send you a thank-you note. You smile, knowing this candidate just passed one of your key criteria.

Then you say, "I never hire anyone who doesn't ask for my contact information. Gratitude and follow-up are non-negotiable."

With that you walk the candidate to the front lobby.

Between meetings, you pass through the reception area. The associate signals for you to stop by her desk and hands you a note from the candidate.

Like a sword from its sheath, you draw the letter opener from her cup holder and with one slice unseal the envelope. The note's contents written in clear penmanship, read, "Thank you for today's interview. Your questions aligned my compass toward the work ahead. I'm eager for the chance to join your crew. However the tide turns, I'm grateful for your time and insight."

The candidate's follow-up is timely and perfect. Now, quite sure your boss will approve, it's your turn to follow up and make the candidate an offer.

PROPELLER PLAN Follow-up with Gratitude

In both business and life, follow up and gratitude carry enormous weight and often determine whether a connection drifts away or grows into something lasting.

Consider these points:

1. **Set a Reminder.** Set a reminder to send a follow-up message after each professional or personal engagement.

2. **Follow-Up.** Write an authentic text, email, or even handwritten note to express your sincere gratitude for an engagement, whether a professional interview, a networking coffee chat, a mentor taking time to give you guidance, or even dinner at a friend's house.

3. **Identify Communication Gaps.** Do you know of anyone who is waiting for a follow-up from you? Even if the window has passed, your fresh "thank you" will positively impact that person, and by extension, you too!

4. **Take Time to Reflect.** Reflect on a recent opportunity when you didn't follow up. What could you do differently next time? Imagine how your contact would have felt if they had received a follow-up? What is your response when you receive a genuine word of gratitude from someone?

Your competitive edge isn't just your résumé or pitch, it's your reliability. Your follow up is how people will measure you. When you keep promises—doing what you say you'll do, when you say you'll do it, and following through to completion—you signal, "You can trust me with bigger bets." Your word of thanks may just be the point that drives home your next opportunity.

CHOOSE-YOUR-CURRENT

As you walk through the corridor, you feel the truth that the smallest gesture of thanks can alter the course of the voyage.

Arriving back at your office, you sit down to type up the candidate's offer letter, when you notice another note written on the back of the thank you card. It reads,

"Send your thanks before the tide turns: brief, precise, sincere. Gratitude is your anchor in a crowded bay, those who follow-up are welcomed aboard."

Choice One

Climb toward the clouds on Mt. Kilimanjaro, where the pace turns deliberate, and you realize the surest way to the summit is to meet each opportunity one steady step at a time.

FIND CHAPTER 18: CLAIM YOUR SUMMIT · PAGE 175

Choice Two

Cross an ocean to Beijing where old and new swirl like a tide on the same shore. Amid the rush and ritual, you discover that belonging isn't found, it's formed through the give and take of every encounter.

FIND CHAPTER 19: IMPOSTER OVERBOARD · PAGE 185

You see a faint pattern imprint and hold the "thank you" note to the light. Shimmering in the sunlight is a watermark of a compass rose embossed on the notepaper. You nod with a knowing smile.

Considering where you will go next, you refold the card, retrieve your "well-traveled" notebook from your bookshelf and place the note between two pages. Tracing the words *Aude Volāre*, you whisper them aloud, the syllables filling you with wonder and gratitude. Tucking the journal into your backpack, you descend forty-two floors and head toward El Faro to pack for your next adventure.

CHAPTER 16

Epic Voyage

As children, we all wanted to be something completely different from what we want now. And even as an adult I'm still unsure if my focus is what I want to be doing for the rest of my life. I believe this isn't an uncommon feeling to have, as a lot of my friends feel the same.
THUYNGUYEN V.

JANUARY, BRIGHTON BEACH
KINGSTOWN, ST. VINCENT
13.2°N, 61.2°W

"Yee-ow! Eek! Ouch!" The volcanic sand burns the soles of your feet like fire. You leap back, half-laughing, half-wincing.

After finishing your morning's work, you were hoping to sink your feet into warm, not scalding, sand. Nope! Next time, you'll keep your sandals on.

Just after the holidays, you and three friends have decided to volunteer with Environmental Protection in the Caribbean, or better known as EPIC, to help restore the natural habitat of the beaches on the Windward Islands. This includes the eastern Caribbean triangle of Trinidad and Tobago, St. Lucia, and Barbados, situated approximately 100 miles north of the Venezuelan coast.

Today is your first day in the middle of the triangle on the black sands of St. Vincent and the Grenadines. The island has a population of about 100,000, and is known for its active volcano *La Soufrière*, which last belched out a series of sulfuric explosions in 2021. You recall seeing YouTube videos of the erupting lava flow.

Finding a spot of shade under a group of palm fronds, you wipe sweat from your forehead. The temperature is a balmy eighty-five degrees Fahrenheit. For the end of December, this type of heat is a shock to your system. Back home on a day like today, you would need a jacket, sweater, scarf, and hat. You're not complaining, even though the bottoms of your feet are now burned.

Surveying the crashing waves, tiki huts with pointed roofs, and hand-woven baskets of ripe mangoes, you watch a group of local fishermen, chatting amongst themselves, lines in the water.

Beep, beep, beep!

Your digital watch interrupts your mindless gaze, triggering thoughts of obligations back home, where time ticks with metronome precision and every second is an opportunity to be productive.

Worry creeps in as you think about the bills piling up in your inbox: student loans, credit cards, cell phone, streaming services . . . your mind starts to blur.

The rhythmic clatter of boats against the shore pulls you out of your head. Snapping back to the present, you notice neighbors sharing banana bread and coconut water with the fishermen. Their laughter carries in the humid breeze. You squint to take in the scene that feels almost ceremonial, each person offering, receiving, and sharing without hesitation.

A woman catches your eye and walks toward you, extending a small, wrapped package of the sweet, fresh banana bread, and a smile. The freshness of the bread surprises you; it tastes of newly harvested nutmeg, sunshine, and unspoken grace. You've never tasted anything like it.

Standing, you walk toward the group on the shoreline. They are mending lines, cleaning fish, and laughing at stories you can't quite hear. Thanking them for the nourishing treat and making conversation, you ask how many fish they've caught today.

One fisherman with a gentle face, etched by experience, wipes his brow and says, "The sea gives what it wants. You don't rush her. She will provide enough."

This is foreign wisdom to your ears. *Don't rush* and *enough*, you've never heard those words used together in your world of deadlines, where time equals money and there's never enough of either.

Here, time seems to move differently, more circularly than linearly. Or, maybe there is more of a respect for the process; rather than the mad dash toward a finish line. Shaken from your thoughts, you hear a series of three beeps. Your friends are vying for your attention.

A text message reads, *Meet us right away at the 'Chill'n Hangout.' We have information from Janus, our EPIC leader, about hiking La Soufrière.*

Thanking the coastal group for your nourishing treat, you skirt fallen bananas, avoid herds of wild goats, and climb the dirt path to the "Chill'n Hangout."

You arrive thirsty and out of breath to find your friends noshing on fruit from a handmade basket—diced mangos, pineapple, guava, and sipping on freshly squeezed juice.

"Where did you get that?" you question eagerly.

Your friends nod their heads toward a group of locals sharing a table where they're peeling and cutting their harvest. Suddenly you are hit by the reality that generosity is abundant and woven into the fabric of everyday life.

A young man, with a smile that looks like the definition of happiness, cuts through the jungle under growth and joins your group. Sitting nimbly with his arms wrapped around one flexed leg, he introduces himself as Michael. He's known your EPIC leader, Janus, for a long time and respects her; so, he's willing to guide you to the top of *La Soufrière.*

His hand finds its way to his heart when he talks about the volcano, giving it an aura of sacred respect. Eating breadfruit from your platter, he spins tales about the eruptions of 1902 and 1979 as told by his grandparents and parents, and finally from his own experience in 2021. He warns that you must honor La *Soufrière.*

Michael draws in a breath, "We will meet tomorrow morning before sunrise, but . . . you can't rush the experience. She, [the volcano], will set the pace in the twists and turns of her path. Only through careful listening and communication with her will you see the sulfurous crater waiting at the top."

This advice sounds a bit mystical to you, but nevertheless, your group agrees to meet before sunrise.

• • •

When I was a kid, my parents were intentional about the giving part of the Christmas season rather than the receiving part. Each Christmas Eve our family would drive through the frozen tundra of Michigan, down a long dirt road to visit an old blind man and his wife. I would always crouch in the back seat of the car thinking, This is the least fun thing to do ever, especially on Christmas Eve!

Once we arrived, though, my bitterness would melt away as hugs were given and cake was served. My narrow focus on my own life widened as we sang at the top of our lungs, danced around the living room, and played the organ with joyful abandon. The evening was meant to be a gift of our time and attention, but instead it gifted me with an understanding of how freely shared moments give value to an abundant life.

During the wintry ride back home, I would always say, "I'm so glad we did that." And I meant it.

True wealth is found in sharing.

. . .

The sound of buckets of rain pelting your metal roof wakes you well before dawn. You feel groggy and aren't yet thinking clearly when you meet the others at breakfast. Janus and Michael stand before you and say, "The hike is off. The path up the mountain will be too slippery."

Your group pauses to recalibrate over steaming cups of Shadom Vinny tea. December should signal the end of the rainy season, but the forecast says otherwise, and with EPIC work halted, all you can do is decide how to wait it out.

A middle-aged man in a well-worn ballcap overhears your conversation and speaks up, "I have a bumper crop on my guava and lemon trees that needs to be harvested, and I don't have enough help. The rain is supposed to subside later this morning, if you're interested." He says it as a joke, but the seriousness in his eyes says otherwise.

Without pause, the words, "Let's do it," shoot out of your mouth with a sincerity that surprises even you.

Both Michael and Janus look at you inquisitively and you repeat, "Let's do it!"

Your friends stand, nearly knocking over their tea, and a round of fist bumps secure the deal.

Later that morning, standing under a veritable constellation of citrus, you are stirred by nightmares of the endless demands from your life back home. Strangely with each pluck of a lemon, you feel a small release from the weight on your shoulders. By the end of the day your muscles are fatigued but your heart and mind feel light.

Intrigued by this contrast, you mention to Janus you're tired, but your spirit feels light. Flashing a bright smile, she wholeheartedly agrees and says,

**"Oftentimes, the weight we carry
is lightened when we serve others."**

That evening, the lemon farmer hosts a village celebration on the beach. Music, laughter, and the sharing of bounty fill the air; gratitude is the chorus. Under the moonlight, the fishermen, the ladies who shared the banana bread, Michael, Janus, and your friends all dance together, woven together by the rhythm of community.

The last song is sung, and you can once again hear the lap of the nearby ocean waves from your place sitting in the sand. This time your feet enjoy the cool sand, and you wiggle your toes to feel the grains. A campfire glows, and your community encircles the embers. There is talk of the harvest, the rains, the volcano, ancient tales, neighbors' care, and gratitude for health. Gazing around the circle, each person feels so important to you now. Being a part of this community somehow gives roots, balance, and meaning to your life that you want to bottle and take home with you.

As the talk fades, the lemon farmer studies the sky as if he can see the clouds through the darkness and says, "Well, it seems the rains have passed. It should be dry this week."

Michael exchanges glances with Janus and then turns to you and your friends. He says, "In that case, *La Soufrière* calls."

At breakfast the following day, you take out your treasured notebook and write:

"On this island, I've learned that time is merely a construct. Nature moves to her own rhythm: fruit ripens when it's ready, the sea gives what she will, and the volcano waits in quiet reverence until the right time has come.

"I've also learned the harmony of community: neighbors who bring supper before you ask, strangers who lend their hands, and locals who share their wisdom like seeds scattered in fertile soil. Here, the concept of 'time equals money' is gently disrupted, replaced by a rich culture sustained by trust and gratitude. It is an EPIC Voyage in more ways than one."

You smile as you write the last sentence and look up to find the lemon farmer finishing his breakfast. He winks, hands you a note, and gives you a hearty hug. Waving goodbye he disappears into the jungle.

You open the paper to read the handwritten message,

**"Slow down . . . time is a precious gift.
True wealth is found in sharing. When you offer a hand,
a moment, or yourself; that's when life flourishes."**

PROPELLER PLAN Nature and Nurture

Generosity isn't about how much you give, it's about how open your hands are. When you pause long enough to notice others, to share what you already have, you discover that abundance isn't tangible; it's a mindset. Every act of giving, no matter how small, ripens into connection and meaning.

This week, trade one "transaction" for a "trust moment."

1. Trade Convenience for Connection. Instead of buying convenience, offer your time.

2. Listen Like it Matters. Instead of multitasking through a conversation, give your full attention.

3. Let Nature Set the Pace. Instead of always moving full speed ahead, look at nature for its clues about life.

4. Lead with Initiative. Instead of waiting to be asked, show up first.

5. Replace Isolation with Belonging. Instead of isolation, engage in community.

Take note of how your inner pace shifts from rushed to rooted. How did you feel when you gave of yourself and your time? Notice how generosity becomes a life rhythm, not a reaction.

CHOOSE-YOUR-CURRENT

While finishing your cup of Shadom Vinny tea, you flip the note from the farmer and are not surprised to see another message on the back. In looping script, it says,

"The island reminds you that abundance flows through open hands. It's never about how much you hold, it's how you give. The tide is rising again. How will you move with it?"

Choice One

Climb the slopes of Tanzania's Mt. Kilimanjaro, where the air is thin and each step more measured, until you see the summit is reached not by rushing past opportunities, but by seizing them as they appear.

FIND CHAPTER 18: CLAIM YOUR SUMMIT • PAGE 175

Choice Two

Journey to Melbourne, a city where rain falls on rooftop gardens and color blooms from every wall. Amid its rhythm, you realize growth isn't found by chasing greener pastures, it's nurtured by caring for the ground beneath your feet.

FIND CHAPTER 20: THE GRASS IS GREENER • PAGE 193

In the corner of the calligraphied note, you see the arrows of a hand drawn compass rose. You shake your head and smile; Grandfather Muse is once again guiding you. Now, you must choose your next voyage ahead.

Grabbing your treasured notebook, you instinctively know the note from the lemon farmer must be guarded for safe keeping. Closing the cover, your finger traces the compass rose and the ancient words just below, stirring questions about the hands that inscribed them.

CHAPTER 17

Changing Course

I have tried a few different businesses, home bakery, online jewelry shop, it all worked well but I don't think it's a fit for me, and recently I took over a business I'm really interested in from a close friend and started working from there. So, I guess, keep trying until you discover what is right for you.

LINDA L.

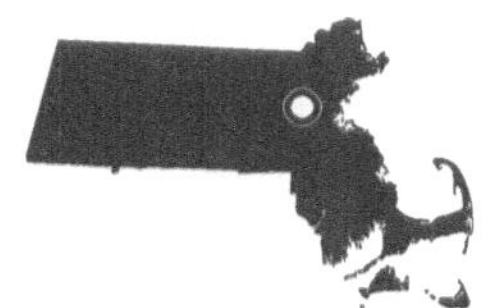

**MARCH, SCHOOL STREET
BOSTON, MASSACHUSETTS U.S.A.
42.4°N, 71.1°W**

At the Bell In Hand in Boston, America's oldest continuously operating tavern, you and two friends clink your glasses together and cheer, "Wicked Wednesday!" You celebrate leaving your jobs and starting a technology company together. Using the colloquial New England slang, this day marks your "wicked awesome" future as entrepreneurs.

You are entrepreneurs and the sky's the limit!

Leaving the tavern, the three of you pull your coats closer around your necks to block the nor'easter wind, and your feet sail across the cobblestones, a reminder of a young America. Passing the Union Oyster House where Secretary of State Daniel Webster was known to frequent in the 1800s, the three of you march down Congress

Street past Faneuil Hall, ignore the tourists at Quincy Market, and find your destination at the steps of the Niles Building on School Street, the birthplace of your new company.

Jaycee looks at you earnestly and says, "We are partners. We're in this together. When the money starts rolling in, we'll split the pot."

With these words, you shake hands firmly and smile broadly.

Jaycee is ten years your senior, a sincere and affable man, well-liked by everyone who knows him. Your other partner, Eileen, is five years older than you, and she brings the operations and compliance background to your trio. You've known both of your partners for five years and trust them implicitly.

Because you've read dozens of business books, you know it takes a long time to establish a company, and you plan to give it at least five years to become a profitable "well-oiled machine." Plus, you're in it to win it, and decide to take very little salary from the company so you can have a solvent balance sheet as quickly as possible.

Now that you have your business license, you are off to the races. In Boston, the Niles Building becomes your home away from home. Each day is filled with outbound phone calls by the hundreds, business lunches eating crab cakes at the top of the Prudential Building, and hoping and praying for your first client.

When you're not at Niles, you're at the airport on your way to see potential clients in Florida, New York, Colorado, California, and even Alaska. After nine very dry months of angst, you finally secure six new clients at once. It is time for celebration.

Momentum builds momentum and you easily secure your next six clients.

Two years later, you have won 200 clients in thirty-six states nationwide and your company is making millions of dollars! Although, there's a problem.

You've been moving so fast, you haven't been paying attention to the details. You trace the edge of your eyebrow with the single point of your index finger, a sign that you are nervous, concerned, and don't know what to do next. You realize you're still being paid the same pittance salary as when you started the company that fateful Wicked Wednesday two long years ago.

After great consideration and talking yourself up, you bravely approach Jaycee about your salary concerns, and he casts you a broad smile. "Oh yes," he says. "We're partners. We're in this together and we'll split the pot once the company starts making money."

His reassurance makes you feel better.

More calls, more business lunches, more flights to far away states, and you garner more clients driving more revenue. You're so proud of yourself professionally, but are growing concerned about your own financial house; you're personally not making ends meet.

One gray, early spring afternoon at work, digging through the filing cabinet for some documents, you see in bold print that each month your company has been paying the mortgage for Jaycee's brother. Rattled, you think, "Jaycee's brother doesn't work for our company. Why would we be paying for his house?"

Standing up from your chair, you walk to the front window to think. While looking through the distorted glass, you see a beautiful, maroon Jaguar park along the street.

Jaycee's wife exits the driver's door of the luxury car and enters the Niles Building. You suddenly have a sneaking suspicion your company is paying for her new car too.

Your heart seizes. Something is terribly wrong. "Perhaps there's a misunderstanding," you say, trying to comfort yourself.

The wife flies through the entrance and gives you a breezy "hello." You don't respond and look back out the window. A tingling sensation ripples from the base of your spine to the top of your head.

That evening you call your other partner, Eileen, and tell her about the mortgage note and car. You wonder aloud what else might be lurking in the shadows of the company's ledgers, noting that every time you've asked to see the financials there was an excuse for delay. Eileen tells you there must be a mistake, and it will all be clear with a conversation between the three of you. You hope she's right.

Your nerves are jumbled, but the next morning you suit up with courage and the three of you sit down for a heart-to-heart meeting. Once again, Jaycee gives you a broad smile and says, "We're partners. Don't worry about a thing. When the company starts making money, we'll split the pot."

His reassurance does not make you feel better.

A few weeks later, Jaycee tells you that he's taking a vacation at his beach house on Cape Cod. Shockingly, he's gone for three months and doesn't return your phone calls when urgent client issues arise.

Both you and Eileen feel abandoned and stranded.

It's 3 a.m. You're in bed, lying in a cold sweat. Suddenly you sit straight up; a piercing thought hits your mind like an electric bolt, *Jaycee is taking advantage of us.*

This time you whisper aloud, "Jaycee is taking advantage of me."

You're racked with fear, bewilderment, and rage.

. . .

Taking stock of my life since college, there were many pivotal moments when I had to make the tough decision to change course. These definitive moments happened for various reasons; sometimes it was harsh treatment, substandard pay, or unwelcomed sexual advances.

While in college, I worked at a French bakery where the owner cursed at me every day for unfounded reasons. He wrote me notes starting with, "Dear Asshole." Though it may sound trite or funny, it really wasn't! I felt degraded and demeaned. I also felt like I had to keep the bakery job because I needed the money so badly. Also, I valued my determination and didn't want to give up easily.

Early in my sales career, an Indiana bank was a top prospect, but in meetings, the bank president's lingering gaze made it clear he was more interested in me than the work. The line was crossed when he chased me down a hallway; I slipped into a room for protection, shutting the door on his arm. In that instant, the choice was stark, protect the deal or change course and protect myself. I chose myself.

Years later, as an executive at a Fortune 200 financial firm, I inherited a team and spent my first week auditing salaries. The pattern was unmistakable: our numbers mirrored the broader pay gap with women earning about 17 percent less than their male counterparts for the same work. One woman, a standout employee with nearly twenty years at the firm, was the lowest paid by far. I brought the data to my boss and flagged the inequity, highlighting her case.

His response, "Her salary is the lowest because she has never asked for a raise."

This left me stunned and furious. I asked myself, "Why did this mistreated employee never course correct and either negotiate a raise or leave the company?"

It can be incredibly tough to advocate for yourself and decide to stay in or leave a job, relationship, or location. My father was serious about teaching me determination or "stick to it'iveness" as he called it, but as I grow older and confront difficult situations, I have to ask myself, "At what point does determination stop serving you well?

Staying does not serve you well when it requires you to betray your values, damage your health, or gamble with your future to honor a past promise. Determination is healthy when your backbone pulls you through hard times, but it turns harmful when it leads to shrinking, hiding, or tolerating disrespect.

Grit holds the line; wisdom redraws it.

• • •

While Jaycee is away from the helm, Eileen and you schedule an appointment with a lawyer for some sound advice. You're intimidated and scared, but feel this is the right thing to do. The attorney sits at his large desk and looks at the two of you over the top of his glasses.

You unravel the truth: years of building and running the company on limited pay while funds were funneled elsewhere. You feel brave and small at the same time.

The lawyer asks you, "Do you have any of this in writing?"

Eileen looks at you, you look at Eileen, and in unison both of you shake your heads "no." You've searched through all the paperwork and emails. There isn't a stitch of written words about "partner," "in it together," or "split the pot."

The lawyer eyes the two of you with something like empathy and says, "I'm so sorry. There's nothing we can do."

Sitting in a puddle of your foolishness, you turn the word "trust" over and over in your head. You had trusted Jaycee. He seemed like such a nice guy. Everyone loves him.

At that moment you decide to jump ship and save your soul and what little money you have left. You must immediately chart a new path before you run aground. The same energy, focus, and perseverance that you used to build this company will help you to find your next course.

You send Jaycee a message that you want to meet in-person.

When Jaycee finally returns to the office after his summer break by the sea, it takes every ounce of your courage, but you tell him and Eileen that you are leaving the company.

With a sudden exhale of energy, Jaycee quips quickly, "Leave immediately and give me your computer."

Stunned by his sense of urgency, you freeze for a few seconds, and then crack through your frozen shell, grab your coat and backpack, and leave the Niles building to find yourself nose-to-nose with Jaycee's wife standing by her new car.

She seems to know the news; probably received a text from Jaycee. Through gritted teeth she slurs, "You followed the wrong man."

After her cutting remark, she turns on her heels and continues to worm her way into the building.

Later, you learn two powerful and heartbreaking facts. Jaycee sent a denigrating letter about you to every client you had secured for the firm. This poisonous act cuts to your core.

Secondly, and most revealing, you learn that Niles Building, the home of your company, was once the office for Charles Ponzi, who is the namesake for fraudulent investment scams.

Ah, how fitting. The barnacles of deception started in that building in 1920 and continue to strangle its victims to this day. You are so thankful you have the courage to change your course before you too are suffocated.

Walking down School Street, you digest the powerful lesson. Approaching the Prudential Building, you ring the elevator to the top floor and take a seat at your favorite Boston restaurant.

You need a moment to breathe.

You've learned from a terrible mistake and, in the future, you will always put everything in writing; trust aside, it's a safeguard to make sure all parties are on the same page.

Your favorite waiter greets you. Along with your usual beverage, he hands you a note.

As he walks away, you take a sip and unfold the paper. It says,

> **"Once again, you jump from the figurative ship.**
> **The sea has tested you before, and each time you rise,**
> **your courage swells like the tide. Cue the Lifeboat."**

This message arrives just when you need it most. Deep in thought, you pull your treasured notebook out of your backpack and scan through all the other meaningful notes that have marked your life's journey. These notes are becoming a roadmap of lessons, ideas, wisdom, and guidance.

PROPELLER PLAN The Courage to Change Course

Courage is not only setting sail, but also knowing when to steer away from treacherous waters. Even when betrayal stings, you are not stranded, you are becoming a seasoned ship captain.

Here are a few gut-check points to evaluate when a course correction may be needed.

1. Conflicts with Your Values. You're regularly asked to act against what you believe is right.

2. Breaches Your Boundaries. You set clear boundaries (spoken and written), and they're ignored.

3. Drains Your Energy. The one-sided relationship drains more than it gives; your weekly energy is net-negative more often than not.

4. Limits Your Growth. Stretch becomes strain; you're not learning, only coping.

5. Takes a Toll on Your Health. Sleep, anxiety, or stress markers worsen, and people who love you start to notice the impact.

The Day One Question: "If this opportunity appeared today, with what you now know, would you choose it?" If not, that's data, not disloyalty.

When someone breaks your trust, the lesson isn't just about loss, it's about you learning courage. You learn to steer away from betrayal and safeguard your future. Changing course is not failure but wisdom; future wisdom to chart bold new coordinates!

Each path lifts you out of discouragement and puts your hands back on the helm, reminding you that even storms can sharpen your skill as a sailor.

◿◿◿

CHOOSE-YOUR-CURRENT

Your favorite waiter signals to ask if you'd like another beverage. You nod, "Yes." He gives you the *okay* sign.

Once again, deep in thought, you flip the note you just received and see another message on the back. It says,

"Grit is the oar; discernment is the compass.
When the current turns, let the compass lead.
Do not fear the pivot, each change of direction grows your
courage and steers you nearer to your true horizon."

Choice One

Wander through the narrow alleyways of Beijing, where ancient temples rise beside flashing towers, and you learn that life isn't found in chasing "what's next" but in standing still long enough to belong.

FIND CHAPTER 19: IMPOSTER OVERBOARD • PAGE 185

Choice Two

Wander through Melbourne's sunlit streets, where music drifts from cafés and every corner hums with possibility. In the shimmer of newness, you learn that contentment blooms when you tend what's already yours.

FIND CHAPTER 20: THE GRASS IS GREENER • PAGE 193

A coffee ring stamps the bottom of the note like a seal of approval. Inside the ring is a hand drawn compass rose.

Nestling the note between two pages of your journal, you scan the room to see if Grandfather Muse is watching you from afar. It seems that way.

Closing the notebook, your gaze lingers over the words *"Aude Volāre"* inscribed on the cover and you wonder about the ancient secret hidden in its meaning.

Looking out the bank of windows overlooking the Boston Public Garden, you think, *This probably won't be the last time I need to change course, and next time I'll catch it sooner and with more courage.*

Steering the Voyage

FROM POSSIBILITY TO CHARTING CONFIDENCE

CHAPTER 18

Claim Your Summit

Don't stress yourself out about what you want to do for the "rest of your life." Tomorrow is not promised. So don't stress about it.

SHAWN R.

**SEPTEMBER, UHURU PEAK
MT. KILIMANJARO, TANZANIA, AFRICA
3.1°S, 37.4°E**

Wedged into seat 94F next to the tiny airplane bathroom, you wipe down the tray table and arm rests with a sanitizer wipe. You are ready for the flight, stocked with everything from your checklist: noise-canceling headset, trail mix, a music playlist, and your trusty neck pillow, all arranged within reach in the dark cabin.

It feels a little like life in Millicent, your van, where you once traveled with four spatulas, a full toolbox, and a decorative throw pillow you convinced yourself "made the space feel bigger." Now here, you are stockpiling airplane luxuries: a neck pillow that works no better than a pool noodle, trail mix with one too many raisins, and that playlist you spent an hour curating but will inevitably ignore in favor of in-flight entertainment.

You smile at your careful arrangement, knowing full well that once your seatmate arrives, your organized system will collapse into chaos as they clamber over you with their oversized personal items. Meanwhile, the bathroom door keeps whacking your left elbow with a grand thwack, as if to remind you: control is an illusion at 35,000 feet.

Your work is sending you to the Global AI Conference, where a former U.S. President will deliver policy and Ed Sheeran will deliver heartbreak, though some would argue it's one and the same. You're excited for the event, but you also know this is going to be a long cross-continental flight.

A crackle gasps over the speakers, and the captain announces in his best Charlie Brown teacher *"wha-wha-wha"* routine, that there is a mechanical failure and this airplane will remain grounded. He urges all passengers to leave the lame beast and find some dinner in the airport with orders to return in one hour once the plane has been replaced. Unsurprisingly, a choir of moans and groans erupts in four-part harmony.

The only silver lining you consider while repacking your thoughtfully curated belongings is that maybe you won't be next to the bathroom in the new seating chart!

Just then the flight attendant taps your arm and tells you that one of the first-class passengers left (probably in a huff) to find another flight. You will be moved to their seat once the new plane is assigned.

"Well then," you respond aloud while flashing the attendant a bright smile.

Skipping from Row 94 to the front of the plane, you relish the fact that you can now dine on the in-flight catering version of Boeuf à la Bourguignonne instead of your trail mix with broken pretzel bits.

An hour later, you're propped up at the front of the plane, sipping champagne with an extended pinky finger and fiddling with the seat remote—part recliner, part Rubik's Cube. One button rockets your legs skyward, another folds you in half. After several failed attempts, and awkward chair yoga, you finally conquer the controls and recline in smug comfort, safely out of range of the bathroom door's relentless jabs.

Now, with the grace of a seasoned traveler, you casually unfurl *The Economist* magazine. You nod gravely at charts you barely understand, radiating sophistication, all whilst side-eyeing the steady migration of passengers trudging to the back of the plane.

Your personal entertainment is interrupted when you hear a voice from the seat next to you say, "Well, I do declare we are reading the same magazine." You can't put your finger on the accent.

Your seatmate is a woman with long, dark hair, flashing eyes, and an outfit of polished refinement. She points to the front cover of her magazine which is identical to yours, and the two of you grin, immediately bonded.

You feel as if you've known one another for a lifetime, maybe more. The plane takes off. You don't notice. You are steeped in conversation about her South African roots, late husband who was a physician, and your mutual love of travel.

In the ensuing hours there are bubbles of laughter, tears of sorrow, and a deep connection in this delicate thing called life. The hours of the long trans-continental flight pass in a flash, and neither of you read even one word of your magazines.

When the plane's wheels finally touch down at your destination, the passengers once again start scrambling, collecting, and shuffling. Neither you, nor your new friend budge. Instead, she looks at you with fixed concentration and says sincerely, "Life is short ... consider climbing Mt. Kilimanjaro with me."

Her words are said with such punctuation, you know she would never extend an offer she didn't mean to honor. She then opens her carry-on bag, pulls out a business card, and presents it as an invitation.

You are too stunned to speak. Between your thumb and forefinger, you carefully accept the offering and nod that you will consider it.

Without another word, she disappears through the cabin door.

At the Global AI Conference, the invitation to climb Mt. Kilimanjaro is playing continuously in your mind. You vacillate between "there ain't no way" to "maybe, just maybe, this is a possibility."

On the third day, looking at yourself in the hotel mirror, you see eager eyes staring back at you, with a hint of mischief that you probably inherited from your Grandfather Muse. You ask yourself a few pointed questions, "Would you regret it if you didn't accept the invitation? When would a proposition like this come again? Could you physically and mentally be ready for a challenge like this?"

· · ·

What do you do when you are presented with a once-in-a-lifetime opportunity?

It's easy to miss the boat while "navel gazing" (my favorite term for becoming myopic). To break us out of the monotony of routine, terms such as carpe diem (seize the day), YOLO (you only live once), or no regrets have become rally cries aiming to empower "main character energy," moving us from the spectator stands onto the playing field of life.

A local coffee shop imprints on their napkins—"Life is short, stay awake for it."

I've wrestled with the phrase life is short. Too often, it's used to justify impulsive choices, reckless adventures or FOMO (Fear of Missing Out) thrills. But a well-lived life isn't measured by how much you cram into it; it's defined by the depth of your experiences.

Living one's best life is not about sitting safely on the sidelines, it's about recognizing decisions that steer your course. Some bring you closer to the horizon you're aiming for, others drift you further away.

When you find yourself at the crossroads of "YOLO" and "Good Enough," pause and ask yourself: Is this the best thing I can do with what I know right now? *Then ask, Will I regret not taking this step when I look back later?*

Making bold decisions requires preparation. When I said yes to climbing Mt. Kilimanjaro, it wasn't on a whim; it was the result of years of groundwork. Long before that invitation, I had been preparing myself: saving money, paying off debt, rebuilding physical and mental strength, and earning my graduate degree. I wanted to be ready when opportunity knocked. Believe it or not, five years earlier, I had written "Climb Mt. Kilimanjaro" on my vision board.

As Louis Pasteur reminded us, "Chance favors the prepared mind."

The same is true for the heart. It's much easier to take a leap of faith, to live with purpose, when your foundation is steady beneath you.

Let courage, not fear, be your compass, and act with purpose.

Opportunities are tricky things; they are easily overlooked. Ask yourself, "When was the last time I felt a spark or my pulse quicken in the presence of an opportunity?"

Think of something that scares or excites you enough to make you say, "Someday, I would like to . . ." What if you challenged yourself to really consider it?

Before you rush ahead, pause and look inward. Does this opportunity stretch you toward who you want to become, or pull you off course? If it excites you, grab a pen. Jot down what it will take: time, money, fitness, skills, logistics, allies. Keep it concise; clarity fuels motion. Then, post your list where you'll see it every day. Let it whisper,

"You said 'yes' to growth, keep going."

Once the decision is clear, take action quickly and specifically. (Book the flight. Sign up. Send the email. Make the phone call.) Small movement breaks hesitation's grip. As you gain momentum, ask, "What am I learning about myself, and how is this changing my view of what is possible?"

Opportunities abound . . . notice, choose, act and learn.

Add meaningful pages to your life's map.

. . .

Jumping up, you declare, "Why not! Why not accept the invitation to climb the highest peak on the African continent!"

Your new passenger friend is right, "Life is short." You know that. You've experienced grief and are now beginning to understand that time is precious. Your days sitting in front of computer screens are threatening to lull you to sleep.

Life is Short.

The date is set, and you have your flight for Africa. The countdown is on; you're in a full sprint to prepare your body, brain, and wallet.

You write the words *Life is Short* and the date of your departure on a piece of paper and hang it on your bathroom mirror as a daily dose of inspiration.

As you prepare for your trip, a dear friend solemnly asks you to spread her mother's ashes at the summit. You take this request seriously and assure her that you will.

The departure date creeps up faster than expected, and you arrive at the base of the mountain more slowly than expected, driving hours on end through rutted roads. Though you have spoken nearly every day, this is the first time you have seen your friend since your flight. Both of you look skyward toward the summit that twists 19,000 feet toward the clouds; your stomach drops, and you wonder if hers does too.

You want to recoil in fear, but instinctively know you must keep a positive mindset. Envisioning success is more than half the battle. Plus, your only way out of the jungle has already disappeared over the crest of the brown and red dirt road.

There is no turning back now.

The veteran guides roll out a paper chart on the forest floor. You kneel before the map in a circle of reverence noting the eight days of spiraling turns up "Kili," as the mountain is lovingly called. The trip leader lowers his voice and waits for your gaze. He cautions with a stiff seriousness in his voice, "The only way you will make it to the summit is to go very slowly."

The guide team chants in lilting Swahili voices,

"Pole pole ndio mwendo."

Slowly, slowly is the best movement.

"Haraka haraka, haina baraka."

Hurry, hurry does not bring blessings.

The guide warns, "About half of all climbers do not reach the summit of Kilimanjaro." He repeats in a more measured tone, "If you are going to be successful, you must go very slowly."

You know he is serious about your speed. He stands up and begins the trek, setting the pace like a wedding march, his hands tangled in prayer position.

Pole pole ndio mwendo.

Slowly, slowly is the best movement.

You go slowly indeed through the diverse ecosystems of the fertile Cultivation Zone, the Rainforest, the Moorland, the Alpine Desert, and the icy Arctic Zone. In the final bid for the summit you begin the trek in the near total darkness, your feet guided by the thin ray of your headlamp. In stunning unison, the sun breaks the horizon and a chorus pierces the silence, "In the sweet by and by, we shall meet on that beautiful shore."

The line echoes through the canyon land, "In the sweet by and by, we shall meet on that beautiful shore."

The moment crystallizes the fragility of life—its brevity, its beauty, its worth. You reach for the gloved hand of your unexpected companion, gripping tight as tears blur your vision. Together you continue the climb, slowly, slowly, step by step.

Nineteen thousand three hundred forty-one trying and exhilarating feet later, you finally receive the blessing of the summit. At Uhuru

Peak, in a moment of airless reverence, over the snow-covered rocks, you spread the ashes of your friend's mother, and your companion shares a memorial for her late husband.

Your Kilimanjaro companion is right, "Life is short."

Unbeknownst to her, she made the harrowing trek up the mountain with advanced stage ovarian cancer. When you hear the news, you are heartbroken and sick, but you are resolved to walk with her slowly, slowly through her final days toward the finish line.

At her funeral, they describe your friend as, "A warrior defined by tenderness and grace. One who was never a spectator in life—competing in marathons, triathlons and summiting Mt. Kilimanjaro."

The usher hands you a prayer card, his arm grazing yours in a quiet gesture of respect, and you note a compass rose pendant hanging from the chain of his pocket watch. In your stunned silence, he gives you a faint nod before turning and slipping back into the crowd.

Your finger traces the line on the card,

"Never be a spectator in life."

Digesting the truth of that description, you are resolved this will also be your mission. You breathe a word of thanks to your friend for showing you this valuable lesson.

PROPELLER PLAN Life is Short … Consider

Life doesn't wait for perfect conditions, detailed plans, or guaranteed outcomes. The moments of opportunity, the ones that remind you what it means to be fully alive, come when you risk saying "yes."

1. **Say Yes.** When an unexpected invitation or opportunity comes your way, resist an immediate "no" response. Try one bold "yes" and see where it leads.

2. Create a "Life is Short . . . Consider" List. Write down five experiences you want to have or places you want to see in your lifetime. Circle one and take a first small step toward it today (research, budget, sign up, call someone who's done it).

3. Share the Journey. Invite someone to join you on an adventure. Even if it's small, connection turns the journey into unforgettable moments.

You don't need decades to prepare; you need courage in the moment. The truth is simple: life is short.

CHOOSE-YOUR-CURRENT

Turning to the back of the prayer card, you realize there is a handwritten note that says,

"Life is short. The horizon waits for no one. Will you step toward the unknown, even without certainty? Will you trust the call of the moment, and go? Claim your summit. YOLO."

Choice One

Hit the road westward toward Moab, paintbrush in hand. The mountains offer a different kind of stillness, and healing becomes your next masterpiece.

FIND CHAPTER 21: HEALING HAPPENS HERE • PAGE 207

Choice Two

Soar from the heights of the Matanuska-Susitna glacier, the Alaskan peaks unfolding like a map beneath your wings, and discover that true direction isn't found in the winds around you but in the steady compass within.

FIND CHAPTER 22: FOCUS, BREATHE, FLY • PAGE 219

On the note, the final "O" in the word YOLO is drawn into a compass rose. "Ah, the symbolism," you muse to yourself.

You open your treasured notebook and reverently place the card between two pages. This message may just change the trajectory of your life.

CHAPTER 19

Imposter Overboard

I am quite nervous about feeling like I don't belong somewhere.
ALEXIS J.

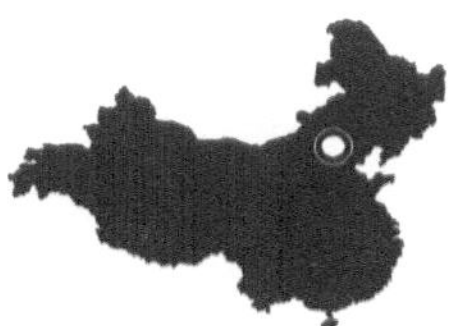

**APRIL, UNIVERSITY OF INTERNATIONAL BUSINESS
BEIJING, CHINA
39.9°N, 116.4°E**

Stuck. You're stuck. Your friends are stuck. The world is stuck. Gloom headlines the main stage and this time around you are seated in the front row center stage.

Your job is a dead-end. You should leave it, but there aren't any other jobs in the middle of this economic gloom show. What to do? You decide to keep working full-time at the dead-end joint while going back to school. You tell yourself: *when all else fails, keep moving forward, and gather knowledge that will serve you in the future.* You've convinced yourself this is the way to go, and you sign up for a course starting this summer.

The class itself is compelling, a two-week intensive course on Decision Making for Leaders. But the real thrill? It's held in Beijing. You're using your paid time off as an investment in your future. You feel a little out of practice. Sure, it's been a while since you were a student, but the thought of stretching your mind in one of the world's oldest and most dynamic cities ignites a fire inside. Rusty or not, you're ready to dive back in.

It's a warm April day and you've just met twenty-eight colleagues and three instructors for the first time at the Beijing Daxing Airport. After a twenty-hour flight, jetlag takes its toll, your eyes feel scratchy and the sun feels confusing for your internal clock. In a sleepy daze, your colleagues load their belongings into the belly of the bus that will transport you to your hotel.

You keep your backpack close so it doesn't get lost in the tangle of similar packs. After all, there is no way you are parting with your treasured notebook. Weary from the flight, everyone on the eighty-minute bus ride is silent except for a set of twins from Texas who are all too eager to chat.

The next morning, still jetlagged, you make your way to the classroom to meet your fellow colleagues. Panic sets in as you feel less prepared than your classmates. How could you forget a pad of paper and pen? You overhear students talking about their scholarships, awards, and honors and wonder how they even considered you for this program.

In fact, you tell yourself, *Maybe you should consider leaving right now.*

The instructor pauses with a lift in his voice. He has just asked a question. Three hands go up.

See, your mind says, *You didn't even hear the question.*

That afternoon, your group takes a trip to Tiananmen Square, the UNESCO World Heritage Site constructed in 1651. You come to realize Tiananmen means Gate of Heavenly Peace, and you feel like that is fitting when you see the scalloped rooflines, calming colors, and the reverent voices of visitors.

Your colleague Anne invites you to sit on a bench and soak in the ancient view. In true influencer fashion, Anne holds up her phone and asks you to share about your first impressions of China. Embarrassed, you shield your face with your hands feeling too shy and inadequate for an interview and mutter as much under your breath.

Anne puts down the phone and says, "You too? Why do you think I'm behind the camera?"

She then sits back on the bench, looks up at the sky and says, "I am so intimidated by you. You look so put together and you have a real job; that's something I can't say."

"What?" you retort. "You seem like you've got it all together."

"Nah," Anne smirks. "I'm just faking it to make it."

Both of you laugh a bit too loudly in a release of nervous energy and cover your mouths to respect the reverent silence of the time-honored square.

Another student sees your outburst and joins you at the bench. He introduces himself as Clark and you think that's fitting because he looks a little like Superman with his air of confidence.

With a handshake, Anne says, "We're just talking about imposter syndrome. Both of us are working through feelings of intimidation."

Your new friend's honesty makes you want to crawl into a crevice in the ancient brick terrace.

Clark nods his head knowingly and agrees, "That makes three of us." After a pause he says, "I think each of us is probably a bit nervous about this new program 7,000 miles from home. Of course, we don't yet feel like we belong."

You are shocked to hear Superman agree with your sentiment and consider the chattiness of the Texas twins as an outlet for their nervous energy. Professor Vie strolls toward your trio to see what all of the banter is about.

Much to your chagrin, Anne once again spills that the three of you are working through your nerves about being in a new situation.

Professor Vie smiles broadly and says, "Ah, the good old-fashioned imposter syndrome. When you're in a new situation, it's completely normal to feel inadequate."

Having piqued your interest, he continues, "Imposter syndrome isn't proof you don't belong; it's proof you care. It shows you're stretching yourself beyond comfort, which is where growth happens. My advice, keep showing up.

Courage moves first, action follows, and confidence catches up; not the other way around."

Looking at his watch, he signals to the group to wrap it up and board the bus. Walking side by side with your new friends, you realize your lesson this afternoon was more than the ancient world heritage site; it was timeless wisdom for personal growth.

. . .

Returning to graduate school after years in a stable corporate career, I felt buffeted by the unfamiliar waves. In fact, I was stunned by new feelings of ineptitude, doubt, and hesitation. Where was this coming from? There wasn't any one particular person or situation that made me feel this way; it was simply an overwhelming wave of inadequacy cascading over my mind and body.

During my first semester, my mind convinced me I wasn't smart enough. In class, I was hesitant to raise my hand and speak up, believing that my ideas weren't interesting enough or my questions too trite.

One weekend mid-semester, I hiked to the top of a hill in my local area and sat in a clearing overlooking the horizon, tears streaming down my face. I was convinced I was a fraud and thought about quitting graduate school.

From that hill, I sent a message to a few friends who knew me best.

They reminded me that growth rarely feels graceful, that the unease I felt was not failure, but the stretch of becoming.

Shortly thereafter, I had a dream where I was swimming beside three enormous whales in a vast ocean. At first, I was terrified by their power, but the longer I swam with them, the more they revealed that they weren't so threatening after all. By the time I awoke, my heart was telling me that the dream wasn't about the sea, the whales were representative of my feelings about graduate school, monumental and intimidating. The dream revealed that I was feeling like a "little fish in a big pond." Rather than giving up, I decided to continue swimming with the "whales."

Once I recognized my own imposter syndrome, I started to deal with it head on. I didn't need to have all the answers, I just needed to be present, embrace learning and authenticity, and accept my mistakes.

Giving myself the freedom to fail was hard, yet so freeing. It was a bumpy process, and it took time, but when I finished the two years of graduate school, I could see incredible personal growth. Those two years of grappling with imposter syndrome ended in liberation; in the end I learned to show up and offer the gift of me.

• • •

Your time in Beijing is passing quickly—too quickly. The course has been defined by riveting lectures, decision tree graphs, guest presentations, and even a day off to tour the Great Wall of China. Day by day, you feel your confidence quietly growing, along with your connection to everyone in the class ... even the Texas twins.

The schedule for your final day is a tour of an assembly plant and a celebration dinner with its executives, your instructors, and your classmates. Standing in the vast world-class manufacturing unit of a global supplier, you are in awe of the precision, care, and attention given to every detail in the process.

The executives are warm and engaging, eager to share their

knowledge and culture. Per the local custom, the tour is paused for afternoon tea served in hand-painted porcelain cups. One executive explains the importance of hospitality and belonging. In fact, he says, "In our homes we keep a bowl of rice ready at all times to share with any visitor at our door."

Thinking about this beautiful imagery, you exchange connected glances with Anne, Clark, and Professor Vie.

Segueing to dinner, your group is seated at two large round tables. In the middle of each table is a rotating tray set with a dozen colorful dishes of savory food. With the rotation of the disc, new flavors and plates appear before you, giving you the opportunity to try something new. In the warm light of the evening, laughter bubbles up and bursts like a tidal wave of energy connecting you to your classmates in a bond of friendship and belonging.

The imposter syndrome that pervaded earlier has now disappeared with each step toward deeper connection to the people and the place that surrounds you. You gave yourself permission to learn and discovered that's where the real mastery of your mind begins. Over the past two weeks, you realized you are not an imposter, but simply working through the process of belonging and becoming.

At the end of the meal, Professor Vie stands and thanks each of you for participating in the course. As his words fill the room, he hands a certificate to each student.

The top of your certificate is etched with these words,

"Confidence isn't the wind that begins your voyage, it's the steady current that carries you forward once you've set sail."

You close your eyes and consider the truth of this statement. Reopening your eyes, you gaze at your group, cherishing the impact each individual has made on your path forward.

You're no longer stuck. Your friends aren't stuck. And the world no longer seems stuck. "Onward," you say, with a sense of belonging!

PROPELLER PLAN Out with the Imposter

You are not the outsider your mind tricks you into believing. The very fact that you question your place in the world, workplace, or pack means you're open to growth. Your courage to participate, to raise your hand, to ask questions, and to try your best, will allow you to fly higher than perfection ever could.

Think about this when imposter syndrome creeps in:

1. Counter with Truth. When self-doubt whispers, write down what it says, then counter it with one truth you've already proven about yourself.

2. Reach Out with an Invitation. Reach out to one person who seems confident and to another who seems distant. Initiate a genuine conversation. Belonging starts with an invitation.

3. Action Rewires Confidence. Even when you feel unsure—volunteer, contribute, connect. Action rewires confidence faster than reassurance.

Belonging isn't a place . . . it's a presence created through courage and connection. When you choose to act in spite of doubt, you prove to yourself that you're already a part of something larger than fear.

CHOOSE·YOUR·CURRENT

While sitting at the dinner table, you turn over your certificate, and just as you suspected, there is a handwritten note. It says,

**"When you finally believe you belong, the world
starts inviting you—to your next horizon."**

Choice One

Drive through the desert dawn bound for Moab. You are stopped in your tracks and learn that healing doesn't happen all at once, it unfolds in color, time, and connection.

FIND CHAPTER 21: HEALING HAPPENS HERE • PAGE 207

Choice Two

Climb an icy glacier, where the vast Alaskan range unfolds below. You discover that focus comes from trusting the compass within.

FIND CHAPTER 22: FOCUS, BREATHE, FLY • PAGE 219

Laying the certificate on the dinner table, you see an embossed compass rose that spans the entirety of the paper. It's a beauty to behold and supports a solid feeling of direction. You smile at the coffee smudge now watermarking your paper, as if Grandfather Muse were sitting right beside you, reminding you not to take it all too seriously.

Pulling your treasured notebook from your backpack, you trace the words *"Aude Volāre"* on the front cover, again wondering about their meaning. Opening the book, you carefully place the coffee smudged certificate between two pages.

Feeling a new source of confidence, you consider your next adventure.

CHAPTER 20

The Grass is Greener

Understand the importance of experience and failure, and don't quit just because things didn't go your way in the beginning. Be patient and allow yourself to truly learn and grow. It will pay unimaginable dividends.

LESLIE L.

AUGUST, 45-MINUTES WEST
MELBOURNE, AUSTRALIA
37.7°S, 144.6°E

Every day feels the same—rushing from one class to the next, hemmed in by drab cement walls, air thick with the hum of electricity flowing through fake fluorescent lighting, corridors too narrow for dreams to thrive.

Nowhere to breathe, no room left to grow, nowhere to stretch your wings. Can anyone think clearly when walls close in? Does anyone really see you? You question everything—your beliefs, your body, and your place in the world. You wonder if the lessons you're fed are truth or just echoes of someone else's certainty.

Standing abruptly in the school cafeteria, you nearly knock over your tray of gray colored food. You've got to get out of here.

Looking for reprieve, you burst through the double doors to the smoking deck, but it's littered with butts and ashes, and the sky the same drab shade of gray as the inedible food. Pacing back and forth like caged potential, you groan,

"There has got to be more to life than this."

You hoist yourself onto a low brick wall and rest your elbows on your knees. Doomscrolling helps drown out your whirring thoughts, if only for a split second of your attention span.

Stop.

You yell at your phone in frustration, "The grass has to be greener somewhere else."

You are met with the robotic words of your AI assistant . . . "Yes, there are many beautiful places with green pastures. Consider: Ireland, Kyrgyzstan, and Australia. Shall I search flight prices and times?"

Your eyes widen and your interest piques. Ireland seems . . . too close. You've never heard of Kyrgyzstan. And you smile at the thought of getting far, far, away and going to Australia, the Land Down Under.

Tossing the idea round and round, you savor it and then begin to digest it. To no one in particular, you muse, "Can I really do that?"

You push forward, apply, and are accepted to a global education program in Australia where you can immerse yourself in a new culture while earning academic credit. This sounds like just the ticket to your way out!

The night before your departure, a few people gather to wish you well as you embark on your new adventure. Though they mean well, you have a short fuse, and everyone is driving you crazy. This just proves you've gotta get outta here!

After traveling backward and forward in time through twenty-seven hours and three different flights, you finally arrive, groggy and jetlagged, but filled with anticipation. Adventure abounds! Let the camera roll.

You walk toward a thin man rocking a comb-over and holding a poster with your name. He welcomes you to the Tullamarine Airport in Melbourne, Australia, and quickly ushers you toward the exit. The sliding door opens to a late August forty-eight-degree chill, and you realize the error of your packing choices. Intellectually, you know it is winter in Australia, but you couldn't bring yourself to pack a jacket and sweater during the 90-degree summer heat you left behind.

Mr. Comb Over, your host for the next three months, sprints ahead not noticing you are fighting to keep up under the weight of your suitcase and backpack. Before you reach the late model Volkswagen camper van, you see from a distance that it is rocking back and forth like the Tasmanian Devil himself is locked inside.

The side door of the vehicle bursts open at the seams and ten kids emerge clawing, scratching, hitting, and screaming for parental intervention. You squint trying to take it all in.

"How on earth do they all fit in that van," you wonder aloud? Somehow, though, you too end up in the jalopy of human popcorn, bumping along the highway.

Above the clamber, the father introduces his family as the Kidmans, then snorts, "We're related to Nicole." He sneaks a glance to see if you're impressed, but something tells you that joke's more dated than his hairstyle.

Just then the van hits an especially jarring bump, and your head slams into the fallen ceiling. Ouch! "That's what you get for your cheeky thoughts," you mutter to yourself hoping you won't need stitches.

The early hour of the setting sun makes you incredibly sleepy, and it is completely dark by the time the camper van pulls onto the dirt driveway attached to a lonely wooden house in the middle of nowhere. This is not exactly how you pictured the oceanside city of Melbourne.

The army of kids march toward the kitchen with empty stomachs, and you fall in line with the regiment because you too are starving. You can't remember the time zone of your last meal—was it before or after the international date line, who knows?

A plate of vegemite sandwiches is served. You've heard about this Australian staple in songs and social media but have never tasted it.

You take a bite. Oh no, blech!

Something about the taste . . . of . . . vegemite . . . is horribly . . . wrong. It tastes like salty tar that expired a decade ago and . . . you can't . . . swallow . . . it.

You look at the little soldiers around the table now on their second helping. The rest of your sandwich finds its way to the dog under the table, and you sneakily spit your first bite into your napkin.

"Alright, enough of this," you mutter to yourself. You need a bed, a reboot, and a new attitude by morning; otherwise, it's going to be a very long three months. Nicole's second cousin twice removed bids you goodnight, and you collapse onto the pillow. Argh! You hit the same spot on your head still sore from the van trip. Lovely.

The next morning you are the last one to arrive at the table and every morsel of breakfast is gone. You are given a sack lunch, signaling hope to your hungry stomach. Grabbing the brown paper bag and your backpack, you wedge yourself into the same corner of the van as last night.

The entrance of the school comes into view and the tangle of the children's elbows and feet surge from the side door with the van still in motion. You decide it's now or never, grab your backpack, count to three, and leap for the grass through the open door.

Mr. Kidman yells, "See you at three," as the van peels away in a cloud of red dust.

Your experience in the van foreshadows the chaos ahead. You are introduced to your high school classmates, but your senses are too overwhelmed to process your new environment.

Lunchtime finally arrives, and you eagerly unfurl your paper bag and immediately wince; laying in a pool of red liquid is your soggy beet and carrot sandwich wrapped in what was once white bread.

Recoiling your hand, the sandwich jiggles and you half-expect it to roll over and squirm away.

You're hungry, overtired, and still not having fun. So far, this trip Down Under isn't exciting, adventurous, or romantic, but much harder than you planned, and way harder than you're willing to admit.

You look down at your slimy beet sandwich, and for a second, actually consider eating it, followed by, "Maybe I should go home."

The five-minute warning bell for afternoon classes sounds with five sequential rings. Unfortunately, you have no better choice but to toss the inedible mess into the trash can and head back toward your homeroom.

In the hallway, you hear someone call your name. You recognize the Kidman's oldest son, and for the first time, he removes his headphones, and with an outstretched hand says, "Welcome to Australia. My name's Chance." His crooked grin looks nothing like his father's, but he did get the lanky family gene.

Continuing he offers, "I just got my truck fixed. Can I show you around town? Plus, that way you won't have to ride back home in the van with all the kids."

He says the last line like a nod to the chaos of ten kids barreling down the road together. The final bell rings, signaling for class to start. You sprint toward your classroom, yelling behind you, "Yes, I'd love that."

Skating into the room, you see a majority of the students at the back of the classroom, sitting on top of desks and the adjacent counters. The apparent teen leader with a mullet haircut and sleeveless jean jacket says, "Hey, where's your accent from?"

You walk toward the back of the classroom and none of the students move.

You reply, "I'm from the U.S."

Some of the students point at others and sneer, "Told ya so."

Another kid squeezed into a Nirvana T-shirt says, "What do you get up to over in the U.S.? Like, what's the thing to do back home?"

The question gives you a longing for home and you reply hesitantly, "Um, there's a ton of cool things to do."

Pausing to think for a second, you continue, "I really like water sports, like stand-up paddleboarding and sailing." This doesn't resonate with the students even though they are only forty-five minutes from the ocean.

Continuing, you say, "I used to do a lot of acting but haven't had time for it lately."

The student with the mullet quips, "We were in a play last year, and it was a ripper."

He sees the confusion in your eyes and adds, ". . . ripper . . . as in fun."

You're shocked to see most of the students nod their heads in a chorus of agreement.

"Why haven't you continued acting? Is the program gone now," you question?

"No teacher. No money," says a voice from the back.

"Well," you hesitate. "What if we start our own acting club? We don't need a teacher or money."

You can't believe the words falling out of your mouth.

A series of "yes," "sure," "definitely," "of course," and "yeah man" erupts and grows louder and louder until you say, "Okay, let's do it."

The clapping and cheers are so loud, the door opens and the vice-principal peeks in to see what all the commotion is about.

. . .

My senior year in high school, I was a walking disaster having been kicked out of class three times—three—and nearly suspended from school, which would've been extra awkward since my dad was the principal! Imagine getting called to the office by your father, who's both furious and filling out your detention slip.

I didn't hate school; I just couldn't stand being trapped in a place where everyone seemed to be following rules I couldn't even understand. I wanted out. Out of the small town, out of my dad's shadow, out of anything that told me what to do.

College was supposed to be my fresh start: new place, new people, no "Miss Palpant, come to my office, now." I thought the grass would finally be greener somewhere else. But turns out, I'd brought the same old ideas with me to my new place, full of excuses and bad habits.

The first semester felt familiar: I still didn't like authority, mornings, or cafeteria food. That's when it hit me, maybe the problem wasn't the place. Maybe it was the fact that I never tried hard enough or cared enough to grow roots where I was planted.

So, I started tending to my own "garden patch," so to speak. I showed up. I tried harder. I learned that you must water your soil if you want greener grass.

Somewhere between my classes, odd jobs, and a few humbling failures, I realized: You don't need to run to find better ground . . . you just need to start growing where you are.

The moment I stopped staring over the fence and started watering what was mine, things started to change. Growth takes time, lots of time; gardens don't sprout in one day, but over time they can become incredibly beautiful, nourishing, and supportive.

• • •

After school, you and Chance make your way to his green, dust-caked ute; a term you quickly decode as Australian for "truck." Though he seems nice enough, you lean into the door of the front passenger seat, clinging to the door handle and your words. Chance breaks the silence by turning on the radio and singing off key to Crowded House, "Don't Dream It's Over." Sorta makes you think about how you were feeling earlier today; wishing this was all just a dream. Fighting a smile, somehow his wrong notes make the moment feel right.

When the performance ends, you take the opportunity to tell Chance about the students wanting to re-start an acting club. He cuts his eyes at you for a brief moment and redirects his gaze out the windshield.

"Doesn't surprise me," he quips. "We performed the musical *Grease* a year ago and it was a ripper."

There's that word again—"ripper." You point it out.

"Oy've got heaps more where that came from, mate," Chance says through his crooked smile, and he pulls into the Big Boss Pizza parking lot.

Once inside, you sit across from one another on a saggy booth bench, and you nearly tear up at the prospect of your first real meal since arriving in Australia. You hope you don't embarrass yourself by eating a record number of slices; but it's possible you won't be able to help yourself.

Chance is a veritable Australian dictionary, and over cheesy bites, you learn that sultanas are raisins, lollies are candy, and capsicum is another word for bell pepper . . .this makes you snicker.

A jumper is a sweater, mince is ground beef, bingle is a fender bender, and dingleberries are dried shit on a sheep's ass. Chance nods seriously like you really should know this.

Nice . . . now, you are laughing so hard cheese is about to come out of your nose.

Chance says, "I knew I could finally get you to laugh. You seem so serious. Maybe even aloof. Give me a Chance," he says. "Ha, ha, ha, pun intended!"

This time you both laugh.

Finally, alone in your dim, drafty bedroom at the Kidmans', you are sitting up in bed next to the yellow reading light. You pull the blanket closer. *What a weird day*, you recall as you ruminate about the wild van trip to school, nasty beet sandwich, noisy classroom, the eager actors, and Chance—a ripper bloke.

Your phone rings. It's 11:07 p.m. on Monday, and it feels late, especially because of the dark winter. It's your sister. For her it's 6:07 a.m. and she is up early studying. She wanted to call you before it got too late. Both of you try to muster conversation, but with the seventeen-hour time difference, it's too difficult on your tired brains.

Your sister says, "I won't keep you, but I just wanted to tell you that I miss you."

Those sweet words shoot a pang through your heart. You haven't seen eye to eye a lot during the past year, and many moments you feel you don't understand her. But right now, you miss her too, and you tell her so.

A single tear runs down your cheek, and you brush it away with the edge of your pillowcase. You ask yourself, "Why did I think the grass was greener everywhere except at home?"

The positive memories of home start returning to your mind like a movie casting images of reality, not just emotions. You repeat to yourself, "Why did I think the grass was greener everywhere except at home?"

Today, you saw your day improve as you put more energy and engagement into those around you. What an interesting correlation.

"What if," you say, "the grass is greener where you water it?" As in, the growth of the grass, or in this case my life, comes from attention, not location.

"What if I stop waiting for people to come to me and start introducing myself to others and actively engaging like I did with the kids about the acting club?

The light within you grows brighter in your dim room, *I guess bad food, annoying people, and bad days can happen in the U.S., Australia . . . or even Ireland and Kyrgyzstan. But, what if I lean in and give attention to where I am rather than resisting it?*

What if the grass is greener where you water it?

Just then a paper flyer sails under your bedroom door and across the wooden floor. You can see from your perch on the bed that it is a paper menu from Big Boss Pizza. Your bare feet touch the cold floor as you quickly scoop it up and return to the warmth under the covers.

There is a note written on the front page. It says,

"Grass only gets greener if you water it, mate. Everyone wants greener grass, but ya gotta lug the bloody watering can."

PROPELLER PLAN Care for the Ground Beneath You

Growth doesn't come from chasing greener pastures, it comes from tending to what's already under your feet. When you give attention to the people, projects, and places around you, you will see them begin to thrive. The secret isn't in finding "better" ground; it's in becoming the kind of person who shows up to life.

1. Identify What Needs Nurture. Take inventory of the areas in your life that feel overlooked: relationships, habits, creative pursuits, health, or faith. Growth begins with awareness.

2. Invest in Consistent Care. Choose one simple, sustainable action to tend. Small acts, done regularly, turn barren ground into something alive.

3. Observe the Change Within. See the results of your actions, and note what's shifted. Sometimes the first shoots of growth start inside you.

Through these exercises you will discover that growth isn't found in distant places or in the opportunity just around the corner, rather it's found in the attention you put in your present.

CHOOSE-YOUR-CURRENT

Just as you suspected, there is another note written on the backside of the menu, this time, more thought provoking,

**"The real art is knowing when to keep
tending to the grass around you and when to sow seeds
somewhere new. Now, the question isn't whether to move on,
but how to carry that same care wherever you go."**

Choice One

Head west in your van called Millicent toward the mighty national parks in Utah, where the mountains cradle the sky and stillness becomes its own kind of medicine. With each brushstroke, you find that healing isn't a destination, but is a result of time and connection.

FIND CHAPTER 21: HEALING HAPPENS HERE · PAGE 207

Choice Two

Soar high above the Alaskan mountains, where the snowy expanse stretches beyond sight and the wind becomes your teacher. You realize that true control isn't in redirecting the gale, it's in surrendering to it.

FIND CHAPTER 22: FOCUS, BREATHE, FLY · PAGE 219

"Whoa, these are deep thoughts for this late in the evening!" Before sinking your head into the pillow, you grab your treasured notebook resting on the bedside table. Before placing the menu between two pages, you notice a compass rose has been drawn on the top. You shake your head and smile.

Turning out the yellow light, you whisper, "Thank you . . . for this chance to grow—no pun intended."

⚓

SECTION IX

The Voyage Within

ALIGNMENT, WHOLENESS AND FUTURE COURSE

CHAPTER 21

Healing Happens Here

*Stepping into the real world you are expected to have
everything together and all your decisions made. But ... life is
a learning cycle, sometimes the plans change.*

ALLIA D.

**JULY, ARCHES NATIONAL PARK
MOAB, UTAH, U.S.A.
38.6°N, 109.6°W**

Perspiration falls from your temples onto the page where you
try to recombobulate your thoughts. You write the date at the top of
the page, July 3. This lonely campground in the middle of nowhere
Utah was not on your radar. In fact, the area looks more like a ghost
town than a recreational paradise.

As you swig cheap swill from your solo cup, you try to re-piece
together how you find yourself alone instead of with your love interest. After meeting your soulmate online five months ago, you took a
risk and drove across the country, believing to your core they were
"the one" or "kismet."

Until suddenly, they looked at you intently and said, "You aren't meant for me. I'm not attracted to you."

They paused and then added, "At all."

That last part stung more than anything. You stared in shock, too stunned to speak. You were planning for a future together, while your partner was planning their departure. You even took another week off work without pay to spend more time together and meet their family over the Fourth of July weekend.

There was no room for convincing. They had decided. You blurted the word "disappointed," but they looked away.

Now, without notice, you feel like you are alone in an ill-equipped boat being pushed away from shore.

Taking matters into your own hands, you jump from the figurative boat into your car and rip from the scene spinning your wheels. The speed of your driving is in line with your boiling anger and confusion. And just like that, your anger turns to great, gasping sadness, and then breaks to fear as you grapple with where to go, where to stay.

Ah, this is how you find yourself at the campground.

Alone. Drinking from a solo cup. In a ghost town.

Throughout the night, there is no sleeping, especially with the sounds of coyotes in the distance and the sounds of "I'm not attracted to you . . . at all" piercing your heart. At 4 a.m., in a fit of edgy desperation, you decide to drive the ten minutes, or perhaps ten hours, to Arches National Park and watch the early summer sunrise. The morning light will do your head good.

You unfold from the backseat berth of your emotional soup, and tumble toward the driver's seat in your wrinkled cocoon. It's possible you're not sane at this point, but you carry forward. It is pitch dark, and you can only see what is in the direct path of your car's headlights. Weaving through a far too narrow dirt path, you find your way to a two-lane road with a sign that reads, "Arches National Park: 5 miles."

When you enter the park, no other soul is around; normally the entrance gates are lined with vehicles that seem to wrap around the earth. In the ultramarine blue of twilight, you see the silhouettes of spires and peaks and guess that your current perch is the best place to view the colors of the sunrise. You feel transported to a preceding millennium, and fully expect to see the silhouette of a now extinct, carnivorous animal searching for its breakfast.

The towering skyline, bookended by stacked stones the size of ancient skyscrapers, slowly morphs to a cerulean blue, the color of your former lover's eyes. With a pang in your heart, you try to push this thought away.

What comes next is even more majestic than you can explain. The shimmering light from the morning sun matches the orange color of the rocks, as if both have been there since the beginning of time. They dance together in a long-awaited reunion.

Time stands still.

The only movement is the slow rising sun and your beating heart. Soon, too soon, campers with sleepy families start arriving, and you know it's time to seal this moment in your memory. You rise from where you've sat motionless for an untold amount of time, and still in a haze, slide back into the driver's seat of your car.

You mindlessly grab your phone to type in an address but remember that your next journey is to "destination question mark." While staring at the screen you see a notification that your bank account is out of funds. A zero balance. You lean your head back and let this second wave of dreadful news wash over you.

"Now what?" You say out loud to no one in particular. Your "soul mate" has shut the door on you, and now your way forward seems blocked. The only thing left to do is drive and hope you'll figure it out along the way.

With resolve, you take the key and turn the ignition. Your ears rally with the startling high-pitched whir, like the hair-raising sound of a circular saw.

Whirrrrrrrr, eeeeeeeeeeeeeeee.

The screech is coming from your engine!

Suddenly, a plume of smoke spouts skyward from under the hood.

In puzzled alarm, you stop the engine and cautiously tiptoe to the front of the vehicle to open the hood. The smoke continues.

You quickly scan the top of the engine mount . . . nothing.

You fall to your knees and look underneath the vehicle, and . . . to your horror . . . you see . . . the entire base of the engine engulfed in flames!

For a moment, you freeze.

Snapping back, your body carries you faster than your brain can process, and you lunge for the fire extinguisher tucked next to your spare tire. Sprawling forward, your shoulder hits the ground as you slide into action like a superhero from a Marvel movie. You squeeze the trigger, and the entire canister empties onto the roaring blaze.

Once the fire can no longer breathe, there is no sound.

There is only the smell of scorched rubber, metal, and terror.

You lay with your back in the dirt, heave rapid staccato breaths, and try to manage the shuffling thoughts in your head.

The fire is out, but you need help.

Rising to all fours, you see a guard house in the distance. Unsure of your steps, you shuffle to find aid. Inside the small shack, a ranger is talking on the phone. Scanning the cluttered room, you see a coffee pot and folding chair in the corner, and you feel an equal need for both. Pouring a Styrofoam cup of the burned liquid, you take a seat on the metal chair.

As you let out a long breath, you see a printed sign taped eye level to the wall, it reads,

Healing happens here.

Your eyes fixate on the sign . . . *Healing happens here.*

A still small voice inside you says, *Listen. This is not the end of your story. It is only the beginning.*

The guard hangs up the phone. Smoothing a strand of curly hair under her cap, she says, "Hello, my name is Grace. How can I help you?"

The sound of her voice gives you a dose of much needed comfort, somewhere between a knowing friend and a wise guide.

"I think you'll regret asking that," you respond out loud even though you mean to filter your comment.

Trying hard to keep your emotions in check, you tell her your whole story of lost love, lost cash, a lost car, and lost hope.

Grace considers your words and eyes you knowingly. Lost in thought, she flips through an outdated phonebook; she's not searching for a number because, she whispers, "It's the day before a holiday. No mechanics work today; not in this area."

The telephone rings and Grace apologizes for the distraction with a look that says, *To be continued.* You again plunk down on the metal chair noting a cold, vulnerable feeling descending over your body; a stark contrast to the soaring temperature outside the hut. Turning your phone over and over, you decide to delete the offending bank alert and see a message arrive from your friend, Maris.

She writes, "How's it going out west? I'm soooo jealous of your trip."

You are uncertain how to convey the events of the past twenty-four hours; a tide of emotions is impossible to bottle. With the hit of a button, Maris is on the other end saying something about how she can't believe you called. The emotion you have been trying to bottle up is now gushing out.

Maris, known for running toward life's snags (in high heels), says in a reassuring tone, "I've got you covered. I have enough hotel points from my work trips to get you a hotel room for two nights. That's better than the back of your charred car. Sorry! It's probably too early to joke about that."

She says in a measured tone, "Don't you worry about a thing." With that, Maris hangs up the phone and delivers on her promise.

Coming around from behind the desk, Grace offers you a ride to the hotel during her lunch break, and when she drops you off, she tells you about a July fourth gathering of local folks at her small ranch and invites you to join. She says it as a statement, not as a question.

The next twenty-four hours unfold in a way you could have never imagined, especially in your dejected state.

It is too lonely and depressing to sit in the gifted hotel room, so you drag yourself, your cherished notebook, and paint set to the outdoor pool. Upon opening your box of paints, two curious children cautiously peer at you from a distance. With each stroke of color on the page, they draw closer and closer, and finally lean over your shoulder.

The parents introduce themselves and the young children. They are from central Europe and are traveling around the U.S. visiting National Parks. You invite the kids to paint, and they eagerly jump at the opportunity with unashamed enthusiasm.

Colors swirl and brush marks etch across the pages of your notebook, mixed with laughter and stories, until dusk. The playful artist's dance soothes your unthinkable day. While packing up the artwork, you notice the children's mother has tears in her eyes. She explains this is the most fun they have ever had, and she means it.

You are stunned by the comment but welcome the blessing.

. . .

Eight months after graduation, I was reminded how fragile life is.

The January air was sharp enough to burn your lungs. My brother and I were driving home in the dark on a nearly empty stretch of highway when, in my rearview mirror, two headlights appeared, too close, too fast. Before I could react, the roar of an eighteen-wheeler swallowed us whole. Metal shrieked. Windows shattered in a glittering storm of glass.

The world spun, and I remember only the sound, the terrible grinding, and the cold.

When we stopped moving, there was silence. I remember thinking, We're alive. We're alive . . . Thank God we're alive!

Fire rescue arrived, red lights reflecting off the ice. The temperature was -13 degrees Fahrenheit. For forty-five minutes in the frigid cold, the heroes carved the car open with the lifesaving rescue tools. They cut through metal, glass, and cloth; steady hands in a moment of intense pressure.

I couldn't move, but I could hear my brother's voice.

Proof of life. Proof of grace.

It would be easy to say healing began in the hospital or even in the weeks that followed. But the truth is, it started that night, in the freezing dark, when strangers selflessly labored over twisted steel to pull us out.

Healing rarely waits for perfect conditions.
Healing begins when everything burns, or breaks, or freezes.
Healing happens here—in the wreckage, in the waiting, in the first breath you take when you realize you've been given another chance.

Sometimes life cracks open or burns down what you thought was keeping you safe: a physical item, a plan, or an identity. The burning is often more of a figurative fire. But I learned over time that life uses these "fires" to clear the path for new growth.

Take for example, when indigenous communities developed practices to conduct controlled burns to restore healthy ecosystems, making the landscape more resilient for the future. Though controlled fires can be painful, they are beneficial for healing the environment.

Ancient cultures often speak of rebirth through fire. The phoenix rises from its own ashes, radiant again. The Hindu god Shiva dances through destruction, not as punishment, but as the start of creation. And in Japanese kintsugi, broken pottery is repaired with veins of gold, the cracks its most beautiful feature.

After the ashes have settled, acknowledge those who offered their support, engage in art or music, surround yourself with community, and give yourself time to heal. These therapeutic activities may not erase your pain, but they can help release and ease the discomfort of stinging emotion. These key elements help restore your healthy ecosystem and make you more resilient for future trials and tribulations.

Healing rarely begins in sterile calm, but rather it starts amid the smoke. Through the ashes, your new growth arrives.

. . .

The next day, stranded in the Utah desert until your car is repaired, you talk yourself into joining the holiday gathering at Grace's small ranch. The rideshare drops you off at the mouth of the dirt driveway, and you are greeted cheerfully by the "Retired Lifesavers," an extraverted singing duo with a long career as local first responders.

When they learn of your story, you can hardly believe how swiftly they jump into motion, instilling their confidence in you and sharing their connections to help you recover from the fire and fix your car.

Following the chatter of guests through the gate and to the backyard, you see a long table set on the terrace framed by sage brush and cliffrose. To the strum of a guitar, more than two dozen local friends gather to sing old Americana favorites and eat a savory spread piled high on trays.

Grace sits at the head of the table. The Retired Lifesavers are at the opposite end. The European family of four is even present, among many other diverse locals who now feel like friends. You catch your breath; this loving and accepting group feels more like family.

In a striking development, your heart is filled with the sensation of warmth and acceptance. Grace raises her glass, uniting the group in a toast.

"Healing happens here."

It is at this moment, you realize the car fire isn't just a loss of metal and memories, it is the loss of your illusion of control. It isn't about rebuilding your car; it is about rebuilding yourself.

Grace stands, walks toward you, and hands you a note. She gives you a wink and is pulled away to another conversation. Curious, you open the note, it reads,

> **"Healing doesn't happen somewhere else.**
> **When you stop running from the wreckage and start**
> **creating beauty from it; through art, melody, and**
> **community—healing happens right here, inside you."**

You read the message one more time and are enraptured by the mix of beauty, horror, and learning tangled in one day. Healing happens here.

PROPELLER PLAN Create Space for Healing

Look around. Healing might already be happening: a hobby that calms you, a laugh that loosens the weight in your chest, or a song that makes you feel seen.

To transform loss, burnout, or trauma into growth, engage in acts of creative restoration and community connection.

1. **Acknowledge the Ashes.** Think about and write down areas of your life that have *gone up in flames*, not just literally, but emotionally. (Example: a dream, a relationship, a sense of direction.)

2. **Create Something from the Remains.** Choose one creative outlet, journaling, music, doodling, photography, cooking, anything that helps emotion take form. Don't aim for beauty; aim for honesty. Healing begins in expression, not exhibition.

3. **Post the Lesson.** Write a short affirmation on a card or your phone screen. (Example: *"Healing happens here—in the messy middle, not after the fire."*) Post it where you'll see it daily, on your mirror, computer

screen, or steering wheel. Each time you read your affirmation, take one slow breath.

4. Invite Connection. Healing is reinforced when it's witnessed. Pick one small act of creative connection, something that restores rather than drains you. Then, share it with a counselor, therapist, teacher, friend, or even a pet. When you are ready to speak about your journey, you'll notice the shift from pain to power.

Healing takes time, often unfolding one small step at a time. With practice, you'll build a toolkit of wisdom and resilience to draw on for the next time you need to heal.

CHOOSE-YOUR-CURRENT

As you reach for your backpack and search for your well-worn notebook, the card catches a splash of coffee. You flip it over, and of course, there's another message. By now, you've come to expect it, but this one feels different; quieter, deeper, like it's coming straight from Grandfather Muse himself.

> **"Mending starts from within, but it was never meant to stay there. What's restored in you becomes light for what lies ahead. There are new shores waiting to be healed by your presence."**

Choice One

Close this chapter of your logbook, return to the first section, and set a fresh course, sailing waters both familiar and strangely new with the wisdom you now carry.

FIND SECTION 1: CHOOSE YOUR CURRENT • PAGE 9

Choice Two

Follow Grandfather Muse as he guides you through your past, sometimes painful memories, and lights the way toward your final journey.

FIND CHAPTER 23: CUE THE LIFEBOAT • PAGE 231

On the card, you notice the coffee splatter highlights a hand drawn compass rose, pointing the direction of due north. Tracing the words *"Aude Volāre"* on the front cover of your treasured notebook, you again ponder its meaning.

You fan through the open pages and marvel at the many messages that have punctuated your journey. You are now a different person than when you began—more compassionate, self-aware, and maybe even wiser. Placing the card between two pages, you close the book and prepare for your next adventure.

CHAPTER 22

Focus, Breathe, Fly

Get out of your comfort zone.
L.P.

JUNE, MATANUSKA-SUSITNA GLACIER
ANCHORAGE, ALASKA, U.S.A.
61.2°N, 149.9°W

The clock strikes midnight. Amused by the near twenty-four hours of light in Anchorage, Alaska, you lift your watch into the air to snap a picture of the hands at the top of the dial. It is June 21, and you are surrounded by broad daylight. In fact, you think it might be fun to walk to Humpy's Great Alaskan Alehouse for their summer solstice party; no flashlight needed.

Winter is just beginning to melt away, but the forty-eight degrees still feels cool to you, so you zip up your down jacket and head toward the festivities. When you arrive and open the door, every head turns to look at you, and in that awkward instance, it feels like time stands still. Clearly the center of attention, it's a vulnerable moment for you, in an Alaskan solstice sort of way.

A bearded local breaks the silence, "Who's the tourist?"

As the music starts again, you saddle up next to the inquisitive local and ask what makes him think you aren't from here. His laugh booms so loudly it causes party-goers to turn their heads your way once again.

"It's your jacket," he reveals. "Who wears a down jacket in June?!"

It's then that you notice he and all the others are wearing short sleeves. Short sleeves in forty-eight degrees, imagine!

Yes, he's right, you're *not from 'round these parts.* You're in Anchorage visiting a client. It's your first time in the 49th state, and you are foolish to think you blend in.

The next morning, the sky is still the same shade of light as it was in the wee hours. You hear at the breakfast joint that "cabin fever" is worse this time of year because all Alaskans are sleep deprived in June. You believe that's probably true as you ask for another cup of coffee, trying to shake off the short night before your morning appointment with your client.

At the office, you are greeted with a gift bag containing a Polartec jacket with the logo of the company. The receptionist says they believe you will need it. You love "merch," but this is also a foreshadowing of the invitation to come during your first meeting. Eye-to-eye with the client, they express how excited they are to host your visit.

"No one ever comes to see us, but you did," Faith says with a hint of respect and admiration. You are quite confident you have just secured this business relationship.

The true test comes when they offer, "We'd like to show you the beauty of our state while you're here, an adventure that spans currents of awe: *depth and distance, stillness and motion, ice and air.*"

You are not sure what that means, but they hand you a brochure, marked with post-it notes and paperclips. It's obvious they have some recommendations. Looking at the pictures of feats you've never before considered, you reply, "This sounds interesting," your voice is half an octave higher from uncertainty.

The next morning, sporting your new jacket, you clamber into a pickup truck with Faith and Max, your key relationships with the company. The windshield is streaked with cracks and crevices from stones that have etched a sort of map in the glass as a reminder of where the four wheels have traveled. The condition of the vehicle becomes clear as your trio jostles over bumps on the rugged road for two and a half hours toward the Matanuska-Susitna Glacier.

The winding road ends in a field of ice and snow surrounded by towering spires, blue crevasses, and swirls of chocolate-colored rocks transported by the ice (you learn later are called *medial moraines*). It looks like you are standing in the middle of an ice cream sundae.

It's a striking moment to your senses. After all, you're accustomed to city life. There are no other humans, no buildings, no civilization, no sound, and no other vehicles around . . . until another pickup truck skids onto the ice patch and an athletic dude emerges extending a hardy welcome.

He is your guide for the day, and introduces himself as Ames. Ames begins untangling a heap of helmets, harnesses, ropes, crampons, pickaxes, and a rack of belays, carabiners, and metal hooks—the sort you've never seen before.

There are three bulging back packs, contents unknown, a Yeti cooler filled with picnic supplies, and a bottle of champagne. Ames winks at you and says that's for later.

It becomes clear that you, Faith, and Max are going to climb to the top of the ice cream sundae-esque glacier. Once hooked up to all the equipment, you feel like an abominable snowman.

Ames looks up the 3,000 feet from the base and waves at his two colleagues who are standing at the top of the glacier. They return the wave, their red knit caps easily visible against the white ice. He indicates that they have already set the hooks at the top and the duo will help guide from above.

Ames then begins his well-rehearsed instructions for a successful climb.

"Don't look all the way up or all the way down. If you think about the whole climb, it'll overwhelm you."

Pausing to see if you've digested the instructions so far, he continues, "Stay with what's right in front of you. The glacier rewards attention. Focus where your pickaxe meets the ice; that's where your control lives. The rest will take care of itself."

The secret is not strength, it's presence.
One precise move, one breath at a time.

"Let's do it. You got this." He slaps your back. You feel your resolve bolstered by it.

You glance down at your boots, their metal spikes gleaming like shark teeth against the blue ice. With a deep breath, you kick—*thunk*—the crampon bites and holds in the ice wall. You swing your pickaxe, striking the glacier with a satisfying crack. Your left boot follows, *thwack,* a few inches higher, as if you are climbing a ladder. You pull yourself up, laughing at how impossible this feels, yet somehow, you're doing it.

You crane your neck to peer toward the top of the cliff and announce to no one in particular, "One foot down, 2,999 to go."

Chiding you with a serious but encouraging tone, your guide repeats, "Don't look all the way up. Focus on what's right in front of you."

You take his words and are climbing methodically as if following a natural choreography, awkward, thrilling, and absolutely alive.

Crack, thwack, clunk, crack, thwack, clunk.

Your ascent sounds like your imagination of a railroad crew building a path of potential to the sky.

At last, wearing a crown made of frozen sweat, you peer above the final ledge taking one last *crack and thwack* as you meet your top-shelf guide face-to-face for the first time. Your movements feel both absurd and sacred as he pulls your body over the vertical glacier face, and you lay on your belly laughing and panting. You did it! You did it!

Never before have you felt so alive, courageous, and proud of yourself. You embrace both Faith and Max, who now feel like fast friends, and clasp hands with the three guides who made this experience possible. You savor what you've learned about attention, perspective, and focus; the rewards that come with being intentional.

You will ponder these lessons for a while, but in the meantime, you wonder aloud to the group, "How do we get back down to the base? Do we rappel?"

All five friends smile at you broadly, and the guides begin unpacking the bulging backpacks.

"Not exactly," retorts Ames. Hooking a different set of ropes to your harness, he says, "This is the easy part. We fly."

For a moment, you stare; the words not quite taking meaning in your mind.

Ames continues, "Your guide will join you in a tandem paraglide to the base."

The red sail and attached ropes are laid out on the ice like a massive jellyfish ready to fly through an ocean of air.

"Oh," you whisper in an unveiled revelation, "this is what you meant by *ice AND air.*"

Taking a deep breath, you celebrate the success of your climb up, but now the glacier is offering you something different: release.

• • •

One December, I decided to visit my mystic friend who lived, quite literally, on the edge of nowhere; a small cabin at the end of a snowmobile trail between a forgotten village and the icy coast of Lake Superior. The place felt like the last outpost before the world turned to wilderness.

While she prepared for one of her healing ceremonies (something like smudging sage, burning candles and chanting softly to the north wind), I borrowed her snow boots and set out to explore. That's when I found the Log Slide Overlook.

At first, it looked harmless enough, just a high ridge of white and blue snow as far as the eye could see, overlooking the gray expanse of the Great Lake. A weathered sign explained its history: lumberjacks once sent massive logs down this slope, rolling them from the crest of the dune straight to the waiting ships below.

What I didn't realize at the time was that the slope isn't gentle at all. The steep angle drops nearly straight down and dumps into freezing, open water. The "slide" isn't a path; it's a plunge.

Yet somehow, this Log Slide reminded me of the toboggan run I loved so much as a kid. Embracing my inner child, and with no forethought, I sat on the snowy ground and gave myself a push. Weeeeeeee! Down I went in a slick skid; no toboggan needed.

I was sliding and sliding, and the wind was whipping through my hair in a tandem swirl of excitement. The ground was as smooth as ice and my buzzing descent was picking up speed. The icy water was growing closer and closer, and I could finally see the drop off into the abyss that would end in a . . . Screeeech . . . While still sliding at lightning speed, I flipped myself over to my stomach and clawed at the unforgiving ice in an attempt to pull back on nonexistent breaks. I jammed my feet into the ground, but that didn't stop me, and the water was growing closer and closer.

Out of nowhere, a long, twiggy vine whipped me on the side of the face, and out of sheer reflex, I grasped desperately at its tendrils and roots. Errrrrrkkkkkk . . . my sliding speed was broken as my hands slid from the roots to the very end of the vine; I was literally hanging on by my fingernails with my toes grazing the edge of the biting, angry sea.

From my dangling position, looking down at the frigid tempest, I knew I wouldn't last more than a few minutes in that watery grave.

The only way out was up.

For the next three hours, I lay face down on that near-vertical drop, whispering the only words that kept panic from taking hold:

Focus. Breathe. Move.

Over and over, the chant carried me—one breath, one inch, one deliberate choice at a time; until I finally reached safety.

Ever since that day, whenever I am met with something impossibly hard, whether life-threatening or just heart-wrenching, I return to the same mantra.

Focus. Breathe. Move.

Focus fades the fear.

Breath restores balance.

Movement breaks paralysis.

It's how I tackle life's hard climbs now, not all at once, but one steady heartbeat at a time bringing me closer to courage.

Focus. Breathe. Move.

• • •

Standing on the edge of the Matanuska-Susitna glacier, you are hooked to your guide, Ames, joined at the hip, the long tendril ropes attached to the red wings meant to support both your weight in the wind. He interrupts your thoughts and leans over your right shoulder, asking you to lift both of your arms and put one hand on top of the other.

In a serious tone he urges, "Now, point both hands to one spot on the horizon and fix your gaze on that one spot as hard as you can."

Once he sees your deep concentration on the horizon, Ames continues, "On my count of five, start running toward that point on the horizon as fast as you can."

"One, two," the space between his counting is measured and thoughtful, "three, four, and five."

The way he says "five" inspires you to run as fast and hard as you can toward the fixed point far in the distance.

You've concentrated so hard on the horizon point that you have forgotten about the ledge.

Running with a massive sail behind you feels like trudging through quicksand. Each step drags, heavy and slow, demanding every ounce of focus. Then, suddenly, the pull shifts, the ground lightens, and your feet begin to rise.

Your guide says as if speaking a sacred truth, "This is where your courage meets the wind."

You're flying.

Enraptured by the beauty before your eyes, your view broadens and you take in the panorama of the sparkling ocean, inlets, rivers, snow covered pastures, and soaring birds. Your eyes trace a figure eight loop, taking in one landscape after the other, sweeping the horizon again and again.

Your lack of fear is surprising;
instead you are reverberating with waves of euphoria.

After a dreamlike eternity, your feet finally reunite with the embrace of the earth. For the second time today, you are laying on your belly, laughing and panting.

After several minutes of reveling in victory, the view, the stillness, and the pulse in your legs, your guides begin unhooking the ropes. One of them grins, raises an eyebrow and says, "Time to trade ice and air for bubbles.

You've earned a well-deserved picnic and celebratory glass of champagne!"

In reflection, the climb asked for more than just strength; it asked for presence. Focus was the rope that held you steady; attention, the anchor that kept fear at bay. From glacier to open air, the lessons are etched in your body and your memory:

Meet each moment with courage,
trust the climb, and let go when it's time to fly.

It was harder than you imagined, and even more rewarding because of it.

To punctuate the experience, Ames hands you a certificate of completion.

It reads your name, the date, and "Alaskan Adventure that spans currents of awe: *depth and distance, stillness and motion, ice and air.*"

PROPELLER PLAN Focus to Fly

When a challenge comes your way, your job isn't to conquer it all at once, it's to gain perspective and to focus. Focus quiets the noise, your breath steadies the heart, and movement creates momentum. Keep those three, and you'll always find your footing.

1. Focus Your Foothold. Write down one area of your life that feels like an uphill battle. Then, name *the next three moves* you can take: small, tangible, immediate. Big goals are reached one foothold at a time.

2. Let Go to Grow. Identify something you've been gripping too tightly: a plan, a timeline, a relationship, an outcome. Now, release your hold, even for just a moment. Trust that loosening your grip may reveal new possibilities and potential.

3. Capture the View. Change your vantage point literally. As you take in a fresh view, make note of personal challenges you've already conquered. Let that perspective refuel your courage for what's next.

Challenges don't disappear; they change shape. Sometimes, the mountain you feared turns out to be a guiding current making you stronger.

CHOOSE·YOUR·CURRENT

You flip over your Alaska Adventure certificate and find a looping script unveiling another note. It says,

**"The hard road is often the truest compass.
Let focus be your rope, and faith your wind. The next path may
test you—good! That's where you'll find a view only
earned by effort. Cue the lifeboat, and GO."**

Choice One

Turn the final page of this voyage and trace back to where it began. With a steadier hand and clearer perspective, you can set sail once more, into new waters transformed by who you're becoming.

FIND SECTION 1: CHOOSE YOUR CURRENT • PAGE 9

Choice Two

Release the weight you've been carrying with quiet gratitude, and chart your course toward the open horizon calling your name. You know it's time to move forward: lighter, wiser . . . free.

FIND CHAPTER 23: CUE THE LIFEBOAT • PAGE 231

Looking once again at the handwritten note, you notice the imprint of a compass rose with an arrow pointing toward due north. You beam at the sign of Grandfather Muse, who is once again peeking into your life.

Unzipping your backpack, you take out your treasured notebook. Tracing the words on the front cover *"Aude Volāre"* you pause for a moment, then open the book and place the certificate between two pages for safekeeping.

Looking around the icy pasture for a sign of Grandfather Muse, you raise your glass of champagne in an invisible toast.

RELEASE
AND FREEDOM

CHAPTER 23

Cue the Lifeboat

A lot of people . . . spend a lot of time trying to figure themselves out.
TALIA R.

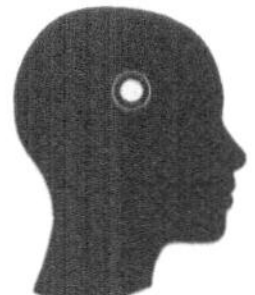

**PRE-DAWN, A FAMILIAR BUILDING
YOUR MIND
100.0°N, 0.0°E**

There is no sight nor sound. You are surrounded by dense fog on all sides. It seems you are floating in the palpable energy of the fog. The edges of a familiar building appear. You know this place well but haven't been back in years, maybe since your childhood.

Your feet move forward almost impulsively, and with each step, your surroundings come into focus. Through the haze your Grandfather Muse appears. He seems to be beckoning you toward a side door; the slow motion of his weathered hand invites you to enter. You don't feel hesitant, yet you understand there is a significance to his summons.

Crouching through the small doorway, by instinct you follow your grandfather without question. Your treasured notebook is carefully tucked under your arm; held as a life preserver. Through a tight, tunnel-like hallway the walls mark your path forward and open to a room that feels cavernous in comparison. The pattern of the floor is familiar. You know this room. It's nearly empty. There are many fond memories here, but you can't seem to remember them right now.

The feeling in the room is punctuated by a stone, spiral stairway. You move closer and gaze toward the hand-hewn steps that wind round and round a central axis, like a seashell with the perfect form of infinite return.

Grandfather Muse looks at you from a distance. His movement is measured and his eyes glistening, almost as if he's floating underwater. He slowly gestures toward the stone walls of the round room. Following his motion, you are drawn toward the curves listening intently as if expecting to hear a message. Approaching the wall, photographs appear as if developing from a hidden source.

Inspecting the picture closest to you, you see captured, in full color, a particularly difficult moment in your life. This is YOUR story, still shots from your life. You hold your breath as your mind unlocks the memory of that painful place and time.

You approach another photograph. This one portrays another raw moment, and then another, as if a guiding presence is trying to reveal to you the truth of what you should now accept. Photographic evidence of your past covers floor to ceiling on the walls of this tight, circular room. The walls rise higher and higher, way above your head.

Drawn by an unknown force, your feet mount the first stone step and you continue to ascend surrounded on all sides by memories, some near, some dear, and others you hoped you'd never face again. With each step, a picture is revealed and a core memory unlocked.

Your once impassive and unaffected disposition grows in a symphony of complex emotions with each new scene. Your heart races, pumping to the same cadence of the symphony. The range of emotions is volatile, from raw pain to euphoric joy, and every scale in between. But the raw pain surprises you. Through the years, in exchange for survival, you have either ignored or forgotten many of these memories.

Out of breath, you stop to lean on one of the steps in search of physical and emotional support. Stuck with your memories, you are unsure how much time has passed; this room seems beyond the bounds of measured time.

You stand, moved by something deeper than thought. You realize your painful memories have been holding you back in your own journey through life. This revelation continues to unfold as you ascend higher and higher. Your experiences, both good and bad, are the stepping stones that have led you to this moment.

**You take the final step of the spiral staircase—
and emerge into the light.
Your own new birth.**

In your line of sight, a panorama of an endless ocean spans the distance; its silver tapestry sparkles in the pre-dawn light.

You're at the top of a lighthouse!

Your lighthouse.

Your feelings are suddenly revealed.

**Each of your experiences has made you who
you are at this moment. The storms, the squalls, the waves,
the undertow, the current of your journey all give you profound
dimensions. Owning every piece of your life, its full
spectrum, that's your true beauty.**

After soaking in the epiphany, you are led to return to the stairway, this time descending. With each step, you face the memories, not to change them, but to see them clearly. Like a reverse waterfall, the pictures project their scenes, as your custom movie.

It's time to own the truth of each memory.

At the base of the stairs, the beat of your heart slows, and blood flow returns to your arms and legs. A long breath escapes from your mouth, replaced by a sense of peace, euphoria. A lightness that you've never felt before permeates your entire body. Almost as if your feet are floating above the supportive floor.

Grandfather Muse is still observing, but this time he has a knowing glint in his eye, a small nod of his head, and a brief smile on his lips. He presents an open hand and is holding something out for you.

A step closer and you realize it's a key.

The moment you take the key the physical image of Grandfather Muse simultaneously disappears, but you still feel his presence with you.

Silence.

In a breathless whisper, you say, "Thank you for guiding me."

After a few moments, you look down at the key in your hand and suddenly realize there is an attached compass rose. The powerful symbol of Grandfather Muse is once again with you.

Stepping toward the exit, your treasured notebook still under one arm, you open the door, releasing a vacuum of fresh air pouring in from outside. It's undeniable, you feel lighter; an unrealized burden has been lifted.

Moving toward the horizon, a vast pink sunrise stretches as far as your eyes can see.

There it is. A few steps away, a lifeboat is tethered to a dock.

Your lifeboat.

Just on cue.

As if a grand director said, "Cue the lifeboat."

You instinctively know the key in your hand will start the ignition. You take another step toward the boat, a step toward hope, a step toward your freedom.

CHAPTER 24

Boundless Horizons

*It's crucial to explore how embracing challenges, learning from mistakes,
and continuously improving can help individuals adapt to the
evolving demands of their careers [and life].*
JANYLA G.

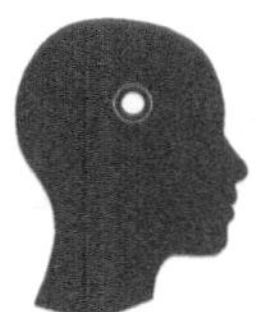

DAWN, LIFEBOAT
YOUR MIND
100.0°N, 0.0°E

With resolve, clarity, and a deep settled peace, you step onto the lifeboat. The wind drapes itself across the deck and the water reflects the rosy ultramarine of the sunrise. You take the helm, the engine key with the attached compass rose is enveloped in your hand. Your treasured notebook sits on your lap, its cover frayed from countless miles, its pages tattooed with a journey no one else could have lived.

You gaze back toward the lighthouse, its ray of light glowing brightly on the horizon, reaching farther than you imagine.

Opening your notebook, you run a thumb over a coffee ring smudge, over the faint indentation of a memory, over the pages warped by the waters of past voyages. It strikes you, how every crease and ink blot has been part of a map you didn't know you were drawing. Between your scribbled thoughts rests a folded note, inked in the familiar cryptic script of your Grandfather Muse.

It says,

> **"Every voyage reaches the water's edge of a
> boundless world. You now rise toward it."**

The note continues.

> **"Step beyond the shoreline and follow the wind
> into uncharted waters, where the pull of the currents may
> take you toward a place beyond the borders of any map."**

You are not the same person as that day when Grandfather Muse first gave you this notebook. You have been changed by the storms you survived, supported by some unexpected allies, and the courage that came quietly at first, and then grew surprisingly strong.

You take a slow breath. The sea hums beneath you, steady and alive. With the weight of the past behind you and the pull of what's ahead, you press pen to paper, and write:

"I've crossed uncharted waters, surfed the rhythm of the tides, and steered through raging storms. The map I hold now is one I've drawn myself . . . not in perfect lines, but in the arcs of courage, curiosity, and choice."

This isn't a farewell to the voyage behind; it's the moment to catch the wind for the seas ahead.

Lost in thought, you continue to write:

"Memorable Points from the Journeys:

• Plot your course and set your sail.

• Ask boldly, listen intently and follow up with gratitude.

• Grow your crew, grow your reach.

• Harness the headwinds to propel you forward.

• Steer with purpose toward your horizon."

You re-read your Memorable Points list and decide that's enough for now. Although, this list may continue to grow with time and experience. Then, you etch one final thought on the page.

"The brave captain doesn't wait for still waters.
The sea rewards those who dare to leave the harbor.
My journey will not be defined by the storms I encounter,
but by the sails I dare to raise amid the rising tide."

With a satisfied resolve, you take your pen off the page and close your treasured notebook. The helm firmly in one hand, you place the key in the ignition. The compass rose points due north. As you turn the key, you hear the words,

"Aude Volāre.
You can fly."

You don't know the source of the voice, but it doesn't matter.
You hear it again, *"Aude Volāre. You can fly . . . dare to fly."*
Looking toward the front of the boat, you see familiar faces from your journey, each one mouthing the same three words, some as a command, others as encouragement, all as inspiration.

As the morning mist parts, you see more clearly the chorus of support standing on the bow: your sailing captain, your aunt, the temple guru, the Zen divemaster, Chance, Ames, and Grace, among others. Each with a gaze emitting strength and hope.

A gust of wind curls through the air and catches the front cover of your notebook. The tattered cover opens, and the breeze fans through the pages exposing the multitude of handwritten notes from each of your journeys. One of the notes written on thin paper is loosened from the pages and floats toward the chorus of supporters at the bow. Standing, you chase the card. In your movement, other notes catch the wind.

Words of wisdom and encouragement, floating in the air.

"You've found your pace, and now you're not afraid to fall."

"Every current moves you toward the horizon that is yours to discover."

"Adventure is knocking. This is your moment . . . You are bold enough to take the leap. What you release does not diminish you; it will make you light enough to rise."

Aude Volāre. The message on the cover of your treasured notebook is no longer a mystery. *Dare to fly.*

The written messages lift, higher and higher, until they scatter into flecks of light. In that moment, you notice you too are suspended in mid-air . . . your feet no longer touching the boat. From the deck, your supporters look toward you in the air, faces alight with quiet triumph. Their eyes sparkle with the secret they've held all along:

You are meant to fly.

Drawn by their current, you rise, you fly.

*Your boundless horizon
has been waiting for you all along.*

This is not the end . . . it is just . . .

THE BEGINNING.

ENDNOTES

1   https://www.whas11.com/article/news/community/moments-that-matter/louisville-tori-murden-mcclure-spalding-university-president-solo-row-across-atlantic-womens-history-month-moments-that-matter-whas/417-19c8576a-d150-48e4-88d1-227f25400990

2   monetizationnation.medium.com/before-walt-disney-created-one-of-the-best-known-motion-picture-production-companies-in-the-world-8a02813ae518

3   https://grandmagatewood.com/

4   McBride, Joseph (1997). Steven Spielberg: A Biography. New York: Simon & Schuster. ISBN 9780684811673.

5   https://www.cnbc.com/2019/04/01/how-oprah-winfrey-found-her-calling.html#:~:text=%22It%20wasn't%20until%20I,fully%20alive%2C%22%20Winfrey%20writes.

6   https://www.theguardian.com/books/2008/oct/11/peanuts-matt-groening-jonathan-franzen

7   https://www.newsweek.com/missing-cut-382954

8   https://www.history.com/this-day-in-history/september-2/diana-nyad-64-makes-record-swim-from-cuba-to-florida

9   TETICS Management School (2021). "92% of people treat mistake as a stop factor." Accessed at: https://tetics.com/it/92-of-people-treat-mistake-as-a-stop-factor/.

10 "Yo-Yo Ma Teaches Music and Connection." YouTube video. Accessed at: https://www.youtube.com/watch?v=dbjgHkj-syM.

11 "Julia Child—Flipping a Potato." YouTube video. Accessed at: https://www.youtube.com/watch?v=k6s6rVAkFrE.

12 Rustin Dodd (2025). "Why Amanda Anisimova's emotional post-match interview was a masterclass in handling failure." Accessed at: https://www.nytimes.com/athletic/6494335/2025/07/15/why-amanda-anisimovas-emotional-post-match-interview-was-a-masterclass-in-handling-failure/.

13 Kieran Mulvaney (updated 2025). "The Stunning Survival Story of Ernest Shackleton and His Endurance Crew." Accessed at: https://www.history.com/articles/shackleton-endurance-survival.

14 Patrick Kessel (2020). "How Americans feel about the satisfaction and stresses of modern life." Pew Research Center. Accessed at: https://www.pewresearch.org/short-reads/2020/02/05/how-americans-feel-about-the-satisfactions-and-stresses-of-modern-life/.

15 Anthony Brandt (2017). "1812: The Bitter End." Accessed at: https://www.historynet.com/1812-bitter-end/?r.

16 "Ton of Goods." National Park Service, Klondike Gold Rush National Historical Park (updated 2024). Accessed at: https://www.nps.gov/klgo/learn/historyculture/tonofgoods.htm#:~:text=Stampeders%20who%20carried%20their%20own,trail%2C%20hugging%20the%20precipitous%20walls.

17 "British Antarctic Expedition." Scott Polar Research Institute, University of Cambridge (updated 2025). Accessed at: https://www.spri.cam.ac.uk/picturelibrary/catalogue/bae1910-13/

18 Scott D. Anthony (2016). "Kodak's Downfall Wasn't About Technology." *Harvard Business Review*. Accessed at: https://hbr.org/2016/07/kodaks-downfall-wasnt-about-technology

19 "From Industry Giant to Bankruptcy: The Blockbuster Failure Story." *InspireIP* (2023). Accessed at: https://inspireip.com/blockbuster-failure-story/.

20 Hans Villarica (2012). "The Chocolate-and-Radish Experiment that Birthed the Modern Conception of Willpower." *The Atlantic*. Accessed at: https://www.theatlantic.com/health/archive/2012/04/the-chocolate-and-radish-experiment-that-birthed-the-modern-conception-of-willpower/255544/.

21 "Work Change Report: AI is Coming to Work." *LinkedIn* Pressroom (2025). Accessed at:
https://news.linkedin.com/2025/work-change-report.

22 Brian Fink (2025). "Your Job Search Is 80% Networking and 20% Applying—And That's Non-Negotiable." LinkedIn. Accessed at:
https://www.linkedin.com/pulse/your-job-search-80-networking-20-applyingand-thats-brian-fink-h6dee/.

23 "Nelson Mandela tribute to Walter Sisulu." BBC News (updated 2003). Accessed at:
http://news.bbc.co.uk/2/hi/africa/3003849.stm.

24 "Helen Keller meets Anne Sullivan, her teacher and 'miracle worker'." History.com Editors (updated 2025). Accessed at:
https://www.history.com/this-day-in-history/march-3/helen-keller-meets-her-miracle-worker.

25 "Mays, Benjamin Elijah." Stanford University, The Martin Luther King, Jr. Research and Education Institute. Accessed at:
https://kinginstitute.stanford.edu/mays-benjamin-elijah.

ABOUT THE AUTHOR

Christiane Palpant, affectionately known as Prof CP, has spent more than two decades in high-stakes financial services leadership. A former Fortune 500 sales executive and current Clinical Instructor of Marketing at Georgia State University, Christiane has led business deals in all 50 U.S. states, built professional sales programs, mentored more than a thousand students, and helped emerging professionals translate ambition into action. Her work sits at the intersection of strategy, communication, and confidence; skills that don't just shape careers, but shape lives.

Christiane is also a professional dot-connector for people standing at the edge of their "now what?" moment. Her education didn't come only from boardrooms and classrooms. At one pivotal point, she traded predictability for possibility, customizing a van named Millicent and embarking on a 45,000-mile journey to paint her way across the United States. Somewhere between mile markers and canvases, this book began to take shape.

Christiane is also a painter who has exhibited her work around the world, with art deeply influenced by movement, light, and the question of what lies just beyond the horizon. When she's not teaching or writing, you'll likely find her mentoring students, in a studio, on a trail, or planning the next creative leap, often with equal parts curiosity and courage!

At her core, Christiane believes this:

Life doesn't follow a straight syllabus. Careers aren't ladders. Some of the most meaningful growth begins the moment you realize you can navigate toward new currents that draw you closer to your authentic story.

Cue the Lifeboat is her invitation to do just that, with honesty, intention, and a little wind at your back.

Aude Volāre.

From the character *in* the book
to the author *of* the book—25 years later.

Christiane as a young student, gathering perspective long before she knew she was gathering a story (as described in Chapter 2).

Christiane as author, at the helm, charting the stories she once lived and inviting you to navigate the currents alongside her.

You've reached the final page, but not the final destination. At www.CueTheLifeboat.com, the journey expands into shared stories, practical tools, and a community navigating forward together. Watch for the companion workbook, future books in the *Cue the Lifeboat* series, and meaningful merchandise along the way.

And yes—this is the part where authors politely ask you to leave a review on Amazon or Goodreads, and share your experience on social networks. You've seen it a hundred times. You've rolled your eyes. Totally fair. But if this book mattered to you, a short, honest review (even a sentence or two) helps more than you might imagine. Bonus points if you text a friend and say, "Read this and let's discuss."

Lift your eyes.

Get your ship together.

Trust the current.

Aude Volāre ... Dare to fly.